MW00877175

COLIN PUTZIER

One Hammer of a Heartbeat

A season on the backstretch

Copyright © 2019 by Colin Putzier

All rights reserved. No part of this publication may be reproduced, stored or transmitted in any form or by any means, electronic, mechanical, photocopying, recording, scanning, or otherwise without written permission from the publisher. It is illegal to copy this book, post it to a website, or distribute it by any other means without permission.

First edition

This book was professionally typeset on Reedsy.
Find out more at reedsy.com

For Janice

Contents

Foreword

I'm not sure I would classify myself as a horse racing fan or even enthusiast; for it goes much deeper. I believe the seeds of my passion were set in my bones and my heart when I was born into this world. I know my obsession began long before I devoured all of Walter Farley's stories in the third grade. I wasn't lucky enough to have a life around horses though, could not even visit Longacres race track until I was 10. I spent my 20's there though, every weekend at the rail or in the stands of Longacres, a racing form in hand and sometimes a lucky ticket.

I met Colin in 1988, a year after this story unfolded. Colin was lucky enough to be born into the life of racing and horses. I was lucky enough to get to hang around with him and Deke back in the late 80's, feeling as if I could touch the life too. I also was fortunate to meet most of the characters that populated Colin's world back then. In our years of friendship, I had never heard this story. When I asked him why he had never told me, he said he didn't know how. Maybe it just needed 30 years to percolate. I'm glad now, that he never told me. I'm glad because it was such a sweet ride to take in One Hammer of a Heartbeat. I have never read another racing book like this, both a memoir and a tribute to horses, racing, and the people who teach you the most. Thank you, Colin, for awakening the images of my youth, the sounds, the smells, the sights, and most of all, the racetrackers and the horses.

So sit back now and let Colin tell you a story.

Acknowledgement

A few months ago, I asked a group of people to read something I was writing. What a group it turned out to be. So Leea, Marlene, Kimberly, Lawrence, Antonia, Thomas, Jen and Jada, thank you for your time, your honest feedback, and for inspiring me to keep going.

Marlene, thank you for everything. You were the first fan of my horse stories.

Kimberly, thank you for getting us out of the gate quickly on the editing and revisions.

Rita, thank you for your encouragement, good company, and fantastic pasta and sauce in adversity. I forgot how cold Spokane could be. Thank you.

Antonia, for food, chocolate, and everything else. Every deer we met on every back road lived to tell the tale, always remember that. Thank you for an unforgettable summer.

Chuck and Cass, thank you for the post-production facility.

Raika, every conversation we ever had was motivational and inspiring. Thank you.

Tony, thank you for the timely inspiration.

Leea, my artist friend, your writing has inspired me to be a better writer, and you have always inspired me to be a better person. Thank you.

Marvol, thanks for the encouragement, and for sharing your work with me.

Lisa, thank you for the encouragement, dating back to the basement window and beyond.

Deke, thank you for Almosta ranch and everything that came with it.

Mary, you made me believe I could actually do something like this. Thank you for everything.

From beginning to end, you were here. I am thankful for every second you have shared with me. A simple thank you doesn't seem like enough, but It will have to do.

Thank you my friends, I hope we can do it again soon.

Arrival

Marv on his good Quarter Horse Blue Eyes, wearing the brown felt hat, and ponying a racing Quarter Horse

The first time I saw him was in late March of 1987, as he was walking through the gate to the barn area at Playfair Race Course in Spokane.

2

He was slick as an eel, his winter coat already shed. He was a little brown Thoroughbred horse maybe fifteen-two hands in height. His legs, mane, and tail were black, and his sleek coat was shining in the sun. He was registered as a dark bay as far as the Jockey Club was concerned, but he was seal brown in color. He was alert, looking left and right as my father led him through the gate, and casually swishing his tail back and forth. He'd seen it all before, and he didn't seem to feel much about it one way or the other.

"Name of the horse?" the man in the guard shack asked.

"Officer's Citation," said the man who had sold the horse to my father. "He looks good, Marv," said Jerry Franklin, a mountain of a man, tacked three and a half, at least. To the uninitiated, Jerry weighed about three hundred and fifty pounds including the saddle, if so equipped. About two hundred thirty pounds more than the average jockey at Playfair. The jockeys usually tacked about a buck twenty. All equipment or "tack" is included in the weigh-in. Jerry was not a jockey.

This little brown Thoroughbred did look good. To me, he looked like he was pretty well put together, but I didn't know enough about the conformation of a Thoroughbred to support my opinion. He was muscular and understated, had a keen head and kept his ears pricked forward, always interested in what was going on.

My dad, Marv, was a farrier but he called himself a horse shoe-er. He was also a construction worker and usually operated a backhoe, big or small, the Case 980c his preferred machine. After work, he would drive two hundred miles or more to our home out on the edge of nowhere. He'd arrive home, bail out of the truck, and my brother and I would find ourselves suddenly involved in a very intense basketball game, us against him.

3

If the job was any less than two hundred miles away, he was home every night. He would usually be up for a game of hoops on that gravel driveway. He always wore cowboy boots with a low heel and a cowboy hat with a low crown; white straw in the summer, brown felt in the winter. Weekends, it was the sweat-stained gray felt, brim curled and worn smooth on the left side. He really wore that hat, and it fit. He wore it cocked off a little to the left, and a little more to the left if he was tuned up with a drink or two. The hat migrated further left relative to his blood alcohol level. His preferred drink was a screwdriver, his preferred singer was old Hank, not Hank, Jr. He liked Barbara Mandrell, too, as far as modern country went, but he would tell you Patsy Cline might be a better singer. "Jesus, that Barbara Mandrell is a looker, though."

Weekends, we'd shoe horses. My brother or I would be cleaning up and straightening the re-usable shoes, while the other one would be holding the horse, head straight as a string and up, still as a statue. Marv would trim the hooves and tack the shoes on, fifteen dollars a head, seven for a trim. It wasn't long before it was thirty and fifteen, Marv as busy as he wanted to be, and then some.

He'd stick nine nails between his teeth and only need eight, every single time. Tack the shoe on and then that ninth, take it out of his mouth to emphasize a point to one of his customers, usually along the lines of Nixon was a no good son of a bitch and that's just a fact. After 1980, of course, the name was Reagan, but the same principle applied.

To be fair and balanced, he never said many good things about Carter in those days either. And while he liked the policies of Lyndon Johnson, "LBJ was one of the crookedest sons a bitch's in history," according to Marv. The truth is, you had to go all

4

the way back to JFK to hear him say something good about a President.

His political views were a minority viewpoint by a wide margin in Whitman County Washington, also known as the Palouse country. There was nothing but wheat farms and fields as far as the eye could see. But Marv was the only union member as far as the eye could see, and he wouldn't stand but a word or two of union bashing before he set things straight.

He was a member of Local 370 of the Operating Engineers, and proud of it. Marv was very intelligent, and one of his friends in the union wanted him to run for Business Agent, head of the local.

"What the hell makes you think I'd be any good at that?" Marv asked Jerry Young, a friend, co-worker, and astute observer of human nature.

"Because, Marv," Jerry said, "You can tell a guy to get fucked in such a way he just wants to go do it."

Marv did have a way with words, as you will learn. He had a way with horses also, a horse whisperer long before the term was invented. He didn't always whisper. A stubborn old gelding with his own ideas might get kicked behind the right ear if Marv wanted him to turn left, but only when the horse was not responding to the traditional cue. Pretty sudden-like, the horse would be responding. Marv could adjust their way of thinking in a hurry, and it hardly ever took brute force. He got on a lot of bad horses and got off a lot of good ones.

The horses he traded only needed to do two figure eights at a very fast walk in the auction ring. The rider, me or one of my siblings, would pull the reins back and the horse would slide to a stop, and then on demand, walk in reverse four or five steps. "Sell that son of a bitch," Marv would say as the rider dismounted, and peeled the saddle off the horse as we sent another short term guest down the road. The good sales sometimes got us a steak dinner at the Stockyards Inn, just around the corner from the Stockland Livestock Exchange on Freya street in Spokane.

We bought and sold a few Arabian horses, imported some wild Pintos from Moses Lake, and even a couple of Belgians from Kettle Falls. Marv had to borrow a farm truck with a stock rack on it for the Belgians. It was a little more than the Ford f-250 could handle. Eighteen hundred pounds is a lot of horse, and there were two of them, one bay and one white.

The first thing I remember about the Belgians, was when we pulled over the hill to arrive at home with them on the back of the truck, my little league baseball team was finishing up a game. I was the catcher and clean up hitter. Not that afternoon, though. That afternoon, I was a surprised catcher who just realized he had missed the game, and it was the only game I ever missed.

I preferred baseball to horses by a pretty wide margin in those days.

The best thing about the Belgians was that all four of us, my brother, two sisters and I could all ride the white Belgian at the same time. She was very docile and actually had a pretty good rein on her. The bay gelding wasn't broke to ride. When we sold them, the four of us rode the white mare into the auction ring, and we were leading the bay. It really wasn't fair to the buyers. An audible gasp uttered when a horse entered the auction ring usually meant steak after the hammer fell.

Buying and loading the Pintos was an adventure. We sold a horse or two in Moses Lake, and as I recall, one was the sale topper, the most expensive horse sold through the ring that day. Whatever the situation, we had sold, and weren't looking to buy. But then these two skinny and wild-eyed Pintos ran through the entrance and into the sales ring. Having been born on the range, they hadn't seen a human being before that day. They were fired up and looked like they might try to jump out the ten-foot-high fence around the sale ring.

The auctioneer had the price up to seventy-five for the pair; going once, going twice, "Sold, to the cowboy, thank you, Marvin," he said, as the hammer fell and the big door opened. The pintos scurried out of the auction ring and into a holding pen outside.

If they sold horses, they knew him. We owned a pair of wild Pinto horses who weren't very big, but when I say wild, just let your imagination go because they were wild.

My Uncle Baldy was there. Baldy said "how the hell you gonna load those Pintos, Marv?"

Marv said,"In a hurry.'"

Baldy loved to tell that part of the story years later, and usually did whenever we were watching someone load a stubborn horse at the racetrack.

"Hey," Marv said. "How did we load them?"

"In a hurry," Baldy replied.

They would both be watching the difficult to load Thoroughbred while reminiscing about loading wild horses in a hurry. I could almost hear the gears turning sometimes.

When we loaded the Pintos, Marv set up a path through the alleyway between the loading chute and the pen they were in. He then opened the gate, went into the pen, got behind them and snapped his fingers. Nine hundred total pounds of spotted fury zig-zagged its way through the alley, sprinted up the loading chute, and into the truck. My brother and I had the doors closed with the safety bar in place faster than you can say loaded. "Come on boys, we gotta roll," said Marv. "Get that tailgate, watch out you don't get kicked." Once we were on the road, the horses would settle down, busy trying to keep their balance in the back of a moving truck.

Only one Thoroughbred passed through the gate, though, the whole time we lived in the farm country. This must have been the winter of 1976-1977.

We kept the Thoroughbred and Marv's good Quarter Horse, Hard Hearted, in box stalls at night, putting them on the nutrition and fast fat program. The Thoroughbred was a horse we bought as a yearling and sold as a two-year-old, eventually named Redda Rosa. I don't remember him as anything but calm, kind, and gentle. He was not much different than any two-year-old horse, just better looking. I do remember noticing how light he was on his feet compared to some of the old saddle horses. Marv sold Redda Rosa and started a couple of savings accounts for my brother and me, five hundred between us in separate accounts. The first Thoroughbred in my life paid off pretty well, I thought.

Officer's Citation was my second Thoroughbred, and I found him to be a kind and gentle soul as well. His pedigree was laced with Thoroughbred stallions said to be of nasty disposition and foul temperament. He was neither of these, and he taught me many things about life. He taught me about the razor-thin line between every emotion in the spectrum, and he showed me how everything can change in one hammer of a heartbeat.

My aunt and uncle, along with my parents, had been in the racehorse business previously, winning the Washington Championship with a horse named Stiltz in 1964, the year before I was born. Stiltz won the Harvest Handicap, and the

Inland Empire Marathon Handicap at Playfair that same year. I used to study the trophy and picture for hours growing up; the "Two Miler" would stir my imagination, for some reason I still don't understand.

They sold Stiltz ten days after I was born, my once in a lifetime horse. I often wondered if it was to pay the bills I created, but it turned out they bought another horse with the money, so I rest easy. Mariah's Best was the name of the horse. "That son of a bitch could flat haul it for a quarter mile," said Baldy.

"Baldy called me from Tanforan and said he was gonna run Stiltz in a claiming race, and they were gonna claim him if he did," Marv said. "I told him, 'sell that son of a bitch and get up here with the money, I got one picked out.'"

Baldy spoke up, "We're watching the race, here's this son of a bitch twenty lengths out of it at the three-eighths..."

"Padding along like an old hound-dog," said Marv. "Baldy look over at me with that eyebrow arched, like..." Marv arched an eyebrow.

"And then he un-corked," Baldy said, shaking his head, "I said to Marv..."

"He said 'Jesus, we shoulda bet a hundred, we'd a had him for nothin'.'"

"Twenty-five to one and run second."

"Big Mirage won seven races for us the next year."

"So did Flying D, they both win seven that year."

"We had some tough horses in those days."

Every one of my siblings was in multiple winner's circle pictures in the sixties and early seventies, but I had to wait until July 22, 1987.

The Putzier Brothers dissolved the partnership in the early 1970s, busy raising families. I was the youngest in my family, twenty-one years old in the summer of 1987. Officer's Citation was my formal introduction to the Thoroughbred at the races, and the first Thoroughbred campaigned by the Putzier Brothers in about fifteen years. He was the entire stable, and his purchase price was eight hundred dollars.

The day I met him, I had been waiting in Barbara's Backstretch Cafe, after going to the race office with my uncle and brother and procuring my first groom license from the Washington Horse Racing Commission. I had no idea how it all worked at the track, and I felt like it would be fun to find out. The cafe was beside the entrance to the backstretch at Playfair, on Haven street, in Spokane.

Barbara's Backstretch Cafe itself came to be kind of a magical place in my eyes, quite a feat considering it was just a small cafeteria with a concrete floor. It was a place where a groom could get a half-order of the Backstretch Scramble, eggs, potatoes, onions, peppers, served with toast, topped with cheese or gravy. The half order was nearly as big as the full order, but for half the price; it was usually heaped high and nearly covered the entire platter. I don't know if the woman who ran the place was named Barbara or not, I just know she called me honey and had a soft spot for underpaid grooms.

I was sitting near the door with my uncle and brother, watching out the window, waiting for my father to show up with the horse. I stepped outside just as they walked up to the entrance. Marv signaled Baldy to handle the business at the guard shack.

The horse walked past, calm and casual, his ears pricked forward; he knew he was back at the track. He had a big beautiful rear end, not at all unusual on a Putzier Brothers racehorse. MD Putzier could put a horse in prime condition, and that is the truth.

I admired Officer's Citation as he strolled by, and walked with my uncle to the guard shack in case they needed a signature.

Baldy had ALS, Amyotrophic Lateral Sclerosis, also called Lou Gehrig's disease. The disease was slowly trapping a razor-sharp mind inside a deteriorating body. I'd seen him get angry about it but never heard him complain. I wasn't aware of how much he taught me about masking the pain with humor. Maybe he wasn't, but he could make you laugh for hours, and dealt with enough pain to last anyone a lifetime.

They called me Bass, Marv and Baldy did. I won't tell you the back story on the nickname, you probably wouldn't understand, and I normally don't volunteer this information. But the best quotes always started with, "Y'know Bass…," so I feel like I should mention it before we go much further.

Baldy and I would sit on the bench at the gap, the entrance to the track on the backstretch. I would light cigarettes for him and listen to his observations on horses, horsemen, horsewomen, life, local and worldwide events.

He'd watch a horse walk by, and then ask me, "What's wrong with that horse?"

I would feel the same sensation as when the teacher announced a pop quiz.

I would listen to the sound of the aluminum shoes clicking and clacking over the pavement as the horse walked away from the racetrack. "Right fore?" I would offer.

He'd nod his head once, ask "Where?"

"Looks like up in the shoulder, but I don't know…"

He'd nod again, once, acknowledging the answer and then would school me.

"Pretty sure it's a knee. Sometimes it's one joint lower'n it

11

looks like it might be."

He watched a horse walk by once; I don't remember the name, but he was never behind another horse for the first three calls of any race on his form. Something Mercury, Mercury something, I don't remember. But I remember what Baldy said, he said, "If we were in this for real, that son of a bitch would be standing somewhere around the barn tomorrow morning."

Then he laughed and told me I wouldn't get far at this track claiming horses from Joe Baze. "He's worth a quarter though, for damn sure," Baldy said as we watched the horse walk away.

Hours Baldy and I spent on that bench throughout the summer, into the autumn. I passed many quizzes and failed my fair share. He called the track "The Evil Oval." His close friends and family called him Baldy, while his associates and some of his cohorts called him Rollin, his given name. One or two of his buddies even called him Rollie.

But anyway, back to the horse.

I don't remember if we had to sign anything at the guard shack or not. I walked with Baldy as he shuffled to the barn, which was right along the outside rail of the track, the stall facing away from the track. It was almost adjacent to the starting point for the mile and 70 yards, and the mile and a sixteenth races on the five-furlong track.

Once that summer, I was holding Officer's Citation for the farrier. The gate crew was loading the starting gate behind his stall for a race. As they loaded from the inside out, the noise kept getting closer. The horse kept getting a little more up on his toes, a little more alert. We paused until after the start, thinking he might break with the horses in the starting gate. He was a cool customer, though, and just pricked his ears forward as he listened to the break, ignored the noise of the tractor pulling the gate off the track, and looked once in the direction the horses raced.

I did love that horse. Memories of his mannerisms haunt me to this day, so bittersweet is the time we spent together. I am sorry, my old friend is all I can ever think to say. I can't think of our last moments together without getting emotional, all these years later.

It is supposed to be a business. You aren't supposed to fall in love. A cold heart can have a lot of success in this game if success is measured in wins. But I don't understand how you can be around these majestic animals and not fall in love with at least one of them. I loved them all, but I admit I liked some more than others, and Officer's Citation alone captured my entire heart for all eternity.

He had 'heart', The one intangible every trainer looks and hopes for. He would give his all, and then he would give more. He earned his keep, and he paid his bills. He filled my heart with joy, with optimism, with pride, and with love. He is the reason I love the Thoroughbred in general, and he is the reason I have traveled through tornado spawning thunderstorms to take photographs of racehorses in the winner's circle.

He is the reason my father and I finally had a meeting of the minds after twenty-one years, the reason we finally bonded, and who we talked about in the hospital the day before my father died.

He was my highest high, and my lowest low.

This book is intended to be about the horse. I will let you decide what it is actually about. I thought I would start at the back gate, just outside Barbara's Backstretch Cafe. The cafe was about seventy yards east of Officer's Citation's stall next to the track.

It took about five minutes to walk the distance with Baldy. Marv could cover the distance in about thirty seconds. He was generally in a hurry.

I can hear Marv now, saying, "Come on, Bass, get that stall bedded." I heard him say something similar many times that summer. I wish I could hear him say it again tomorrow, over the sound of muted hoofbeats coming out of the fog early in the morning, on the backstretch.

Pedigree

Tom Rolfe, winner of the 1965 Preakness Stakes, and great grandsire of Officer's Citation

Officer's Citation was pretty well bred for an eight hundred dollar racehorse. At least I thought he was.

In just the thirty years since he raced, the gene pool has shrunk considerably. The trends in the breeding industry have been exclusively about speed. This has been slowly strangling the bloodlines of the stayers and the professionals, the horses who run the route races, further than the classic distance of a mile and a quarter. It goes a long way toward explaining why there was a thirty-seven-year drought between Triple Crown winners Affirmed in 1978 and American Pharoah in 2015.

Officer's Citation's pedigree had its fair share of famous names. In the fourth generation of his pedigree, the names of the stallions are Ribot, War Admiral, Nasrullah, Hill Prince, Bull Dog, Hyperion, Shannon, and War Admiral once again.

All of these stallions with the exceptions of Shannon and Hill Prince have attained Chef de Race status, a designation for stallions who have been influential on the breed as a whole.

The Chef's de Race stallions are assigned letters designating the characteristics they are likely to pass on to their progeny, where speed and stamina is concerned.

The designations, from sprint to route, are brilliant, intermediate, classic, solid, and professional. A brilliant sire will transmit sprinting speed to his progeny, a professional will transmit stamina. Intermediate, Classic, and Solid are designations for progressively longer distances between brilliant and professional. The classic distance is a mile and a quarter, the distance at which the Kentucky Derby and the Breeders Cup Classic are run.

The Belmont Stakes is now the longest dirt track graded stakes race in North America at a mile and a half. It is referred to as the test of champions, and more often than not, is the graveyard for dreams of immortality. The Derby will get you into the history books, but only the Triple Crown guarantees immortality.

The number of times a Chef de Race sire's transmittable characteristics appear in a horses pedigree are counted, weighted, and arranged into what is called a dosage profile. The weighting is sixteen points in the first generation, eight in the second, four in the third, and two in the fourth, assuming the influence of the stallion is less the further back in the pedigree you go. The first four generations are the important ones, the 'engine room'. So Man O' War doesn't really factor, but his son, War Admiral does. War Admiral brings the resume of a heavyweight, as he was Man O'War's leading earner on the track, a Triple Crown Winner, and Chef de Race with a classic designation. He is probably most famous among casual fans for losing his match race with Seabiscuit, as documented in the movie "Seabiscuit," in my opinion one of the more realistic depictions of life on the racetrack according to Hollywood.

Officer's Citation's dosage profile was 11-6-12-0-3 (32) DI = 2.56 CD = 0.69

DI is dosage index, Officer's Citation's index indicating that he had two and a half times more speed than stamina in his pedigree. CD is center of distribution. His center of distribution index was on the intermediate side of classic, meaning that his likely best distance was a mile to a mile and an eighth.

By comparison, Seattle Slews dosage profile was 7-6-4-5-0 (22) DI = 2.14 CD = 0.68, indicating that Officer's Citation could run a little faster and a little further than Seattle Slew. In reality, Seattle Slew was a Triple Crown winner worth millions, while Officer's Citation, was a horse who had never won two races, worth eight hundred dollars. On his best day, Officer's Citation could not run fast enough to lead Seattle Slew to the starting gate.

All of these numbers and characteristics matter in the auction ring, none of them matter on the track. The horse is what he is. The point to the exercise is that they are all royalty to some degree, at least on paper. There are many philosophies on breeding, but you just don't know if the foal can run or not until they spring the latch on the starting gate. There are many reasons the homestretch is called heartbreak lane.

A friend of mine named Jens Pulver, a retired jockey and trainer, once told me he asked someone from one of the big Kentucky breeding farms how they knew who the good ones were when they were colts. The breeder said, "We take that Cadillac out in the pasture and chase them around, and say 'hey, that one is pretty quick'." Jens wasn't sure if he believed him or not. Jens himself was a sire of note, siring Jens Pulver Jr., also known as 'Little Evil' to ultimate fighting fans.

At the track, both people and horses had a sire and a dam. For instance, there were two jockeys, Arthur and Richard Ochoa, and Arthur's agent was a crony of Baldy's.

Baldy asked, "Is Arthur by the same sire as Richard?"

Russ, his buddy, responded, "I believe they are full brothers."

Meaning they also had the same dam, obviously. Pedigree is important at the racetrack.

Nearly every registered Thoroughbred today can trace his tail-male ancestry to one stallion, The Darley Arabian, through a legendary Stallion named Eclipse. The Thoroughbred championships are known collectively as the Eclipse awards. Originally, the breed was started with four foundation Sires, but at least two of the other lines are extinct as far as tail male, (the top line in the pedigree, the "sire line"), and if the other still exists, it is on an irreversible path to extinction.

If someone were to ask how Officer's Citation was bred, you might say he's Ribot, and four by four to War Admiral. Ribot was tail male, or Officer's Citation's paternal great, great, grandsire, and War Admiral appears twice in the fourth generation. More accurately, you would say Flag Officer, out of a Citation mare; and if you were trying to sell him, you might say he was four by four to War Admiral.

Ribot was the creation of the eccentric Italian Senator and horse breeder, Frederico Tesio, the mad scientist of Thoroughbred breeding. Ribot was the superhorse of his generation. He was a two-time winner of the Prix de l'Arc de Triomphe, retired undefeated at 5, and is a racehorse you could make a case for as greatest of all time. It is said that Ribot was Tesio's perfect creation. Tesio did not see him race but died when Ribot was a yearling.

Tesio, however, was also the breeder of a stallion named Nearco, who is a primary influence today in North American racing. If you were to throw a rock at a heard of Thoroughbreds, you would hit something related to Nearco.

You shouldn't throw rocks at Thoroughbreds, ever. Maybe go pet one instead, he will be related to Nearco.

Nearco is the point stallion to Seattle Slew, one of the most prolific modern sires of the breed. Nearco is also the point stallion to the Bold Ruler, Hail to Reason/Turn To, and Northern Dancer sire lines. These sire lines encompass a huge swath of the modern Thoroughbred pedigree.

I once read a book written by Tesio, his thoughts on breeding and the breed. It is not a blueprint. It is actually more of a treasure map, where you have to search through his many observations for secrets to his success. He went against the conventional wisdom of his day and put his stamp on the Thoroughbred for all time. The book is called "In His Own Words", and is a must-read for anyone interested in the Thoroughbred.

Nearco was represented in Officer's Citations pedigree by Nasrullah, the sire of Bold Ruler, and the Grandsire of Secretariat, great grandsire of Seattle Slew, and the Dominant line in racing today. Bold Ruler was the broodmare sire to Flag Officer, the sire of Officer's Citation.

Tom Rolfe, the winner of the 1965 Preakness Stakes, was the son of Ribot, his leading earner on the track, and attained Chef de Race (French for chiefs of the breed) with a classic professional designation, meaning he was a stamina influence. The direct sire line to Tom Rolfe, if active today, is barely a trickle, the modern breeders breeding away from stamina. He may still be represented through Hoist the Flag, but you would be surprised to see how fast a sire line can die off. Tom Rolfe was Officer's Citation's great grandsire.

The Ribot sire line lives on today through his son Graustark and thrives on the track today. The Ribots had speed as well as stamina.

Tom Rolfe's son was Hoist the Flag, champion two-year-old colt. Said to have had a fearsome disposition, he never finished behind another horse in six starts. He won five of them, and his lone loss was when he was controversially disqualified from his victory in the Champagne Stakes. He was the Grandsire of Officer's Citation. He was Chef de Race with a brilliant intermediate designation, a speed influence.

"Hoist The Flag was a running son of a bitch," said Baldy. "But he broke a hind leg a month before the Derby. Otherwise, he'd have won it. From what I hear, they were damn lucky to save his life."

His son was Flag Officer, winner of the Illinois Derby and imported to stand at stud in Washington state when his race career ended. He sired some tough horses, who got tougher as the track got muddier and the distances got longer. His best offspring were all fillies, and his leading money earner made a quarter of a million dollars. He was the sire of Officer's Citation.

Citation, another for whom you could make a strong case for greatest Thoroughbred racehorse of all time, never attained Chef de Race. He appeared in the second generation of Officer's Citation's pedigree, as his broodmare sire, or maternal grandsire.

Officer's Citation was inbred Four by four to War Admiral, meaning twice in the fourth generation, making War Admiral the most prominent name in the pedigree, but not necessarily the most influential.

We tend to study stallions more, but the bottom side of the pedigree, the family line, has a huge influence. I would go into this further, but you could fill up a set of encyclopedias with a dissertation on both the top and bottom sides of the Thoroughbred pedigree, so I won't.

But I would study Officer's Citation's pedigree for hours, and tell him about his famous ancestors and the famous races they had won. He was a kind horse, never kicked, never bit. Both War Admiral and Ribot were known to be fire breathing dragons on and off the track, and so was Hoist the Flag.

You just don't know exactly what characteristics will be transmitted in the breeding shed, but you hope for good conformation and heart. The faster they are, the more you tolerate. The idea at the races is to give them the mentality of a schoolyard bully, relaxed, but on the muscle as a course of habit.

You can spend a fortune breeding, or you can wait until the end of their three-year-old year, and buy one you think you can help for eight hundred dollars. That is what they used to do, the Putzier Brothers. First, find a sound but sour horse, and buy them cheap. Then, change their program enough to win races thirty days after the purchase, or better yet, winter them and bring them back fresh, fat, and ready.

Many of the winner's circle pictures at home were of horses whose career had come back to life after a dry spell in the previous stable. Usually, you would see a complete reversal of form after only thirty days in the Putzier Brother's barn. They weren't miracle workers, but they could get a horse to perform to its potential.

My father would tell me which horses could be had cheap, and who he could improve. You could usually make money gambling on his horses no later than the second start under the white silks of the Putzier Brothers, often the first.

They never put the horses on, and usually took them off all medications, except for a race day painkiller called Butazolidin. Starting day one, we poured the grain, vitamins, and supplements to the horse. We fed way more than most on the backstretch, giving them all the grain they would clean up. Once they started training and racing, the trick was to keep them in the feed tub.

"What you do, Bass," said Marv, "you take a worn out little son of a bitch ain't had a day off in his life, put a poultice on his heart, and about the time he gets too tough to handle, you enter him."

They had a way with words, the Putzier Brothers. They had a way with horses as well, and the system worked. I was about to get a great education from a couple of great horsemen. We moved in and settled into life at the track. It was all new to me on the backstretch. I had distant memories of the place from when I was a toddler but had been relegated to the grandstand side of the track from the ages of six to twenty.

I remembered it as a wondrous place then, the smells and sounds of the backstretch, the steam coming off the horses after their workout in the chilly morning air. I still remember it as a wondrous place. There is nothing like the backstretch on Saturday morning, whether you have a horse or not.

I never learned to fish much, growing up. If we were up that early, we were at a horse event, auction, or race track. Looking back, It was absolutely the right choice, my thoughts at the time notwithstanding.

The first two weeks of training, Officer's Citation was led around the track at a slow gallop, with no tack, just a halter. A man we knew as Bux would take the horse to the track. Bux, mounted on a big quarter horse, would lead Officer's Citation, just loping along for two circuits, about a mile and a quarter, depending upon where they started and where they finished.

When coming off the track, the riders would pull the horse up near the gap. They would then turn to face the track and come to a stop. They would pause a moment before turning and leaving the track. This is so the horses don't get in the habit of running off the track through the gap when they are through.

It is also a photograph in my mind, the Thoroughbred turning toward the track, his ears pricked forward and his intelligent eyes surveying the scene of his domain. A little thing that can take your breath away, if you aren't careful.

Baldy, my brother Deke, and I would watch Officer's Citation jog on the track as Bux led him. Afterward, my brother and I would cool the horse out, clean his stall, and fill his hay net and water bucket. We would then toss him some grain, go to work at our day jobs on weekdays, or loiter around the backstretch on weekends.

Sometimes I would study the racing form at Barbara's Backstretch Cafe, or sometimes I would go to the guinea stand to watch the horses, and listen to the trainers. I could stand next to the rail, watch the horses jog by the wrong way against the outside rail heading up the track to where they would stop, turn, and begin to jog as they accelerated into a slow or fast gallop, sometimes going for a timed workout.

The rider would always stop the horse before going on to the next part of the routine, rather than just turning into the workout. It was difficult to control a horse riding a flat saddle, and it was a fine line keeping a horse on the razor's edge of exploding and still convinced that he could be controlled. It was important to never be in too much of a hurry.

The flat saddle is all about leverage and balance. There is nothing much to hold on to, and when the horse blows up on the track and starts raising hell, your options quickly dwindle. Leverage is replaced by prayer when the horse rears up, and balance and hope usually go out the window at the same time, shortly before you learn exactly how deep, and how hard the track is today.

The primary goal in these situations is to hold on to the reins if you are thrown so the horse won't run off and hurt himself. Of secondary importance is to not get yourself killed. Unwritten rules, but rules nonetheless.

We galloped Officer's Citation slow, as slow as a horse could gallop, and we had a gallop boy who had worked with my uncle for many years at the track. Leonard was quiet and very good with horses. He knew what Baldy wanted, knew how to interpret his wicked sense of humor, and he could get a horse to relax.

The purpose of the slow gallop was twofold, to build muscle using isometrics, and to keep his legs under him, keep him sound and healthy. You could bow a tendon on a horse if you galloped too fast too often, or trained too aggressively and worked the horse too often.

Bowing a tendon means that the supporting structure that held the tendon against the back of the shin bone would rupture, forming a bow with the tendon behind the lower front leg or legs. It took a horse at least a year, if at all, to recover from a bowed tendon. The Putzier brothers never bowed a tendon in all their years of racing.

Bowed tendons are the main reason many potential champions were forced into early retirement. The most recent famous example I can think of would be I'll Have Another being scratched two days before the Belmont Stakes in 2012, having already won the first two legs of the Triple Crown. His training regimen consisted of fast gallops, sometimes called a two-minute lick, meaning a pace that would cover a mile in two minutes.

"Don't ever two-minute lick a horse unless you want to own a cripple," Baldy would tell me. I have never been a licensed trainer, and have no business second-guessing a trainer who makes noise in the national standings. But according to Marv and Baldy, slow gallops were all that was needed, and I have never found a reason to doubt them.

Better horses will stand up to more training, and, in fact, sometimes demand it. The bowed tendon is the penalty for taking your horse to the track once too often. The only positive thing to be said about a bow is that they are usually not life-threatening.

A trainer friend of Baldy's came up with a pretty good method for rehabilitating a bow. "It's because he keeps crippling his horses," Baldy said. "He gallops fast, works fast from the gate. That's how he bows horses. If he doesn't change his methods, he'll get a chance to rehabilitate a lot of them."

I believed Baldy. He was a pretty keen observer of what went on at the gap.

"But he's on to something," Baldy said. "It seems like the sooner you can get them walking and active, the quicker they heal."

You paid five dollars for a gallop, so most riders preferred to go fast. More horses galloped meant more money, and you couldn't blame the riders for wanting to go fast. It was good having someone like Leonard available. We were building a foundation under Officer's Citation, and it was going to take some time.

Settling In

The grandstand viewed from the clubhouse turn

I was settling in, getting used to the routine at the track. I was happy to be there, forming a good relationship with the horse, and learning. It was interesting, it was fun, and it was a great place to be, but it still hadn't stirred my imagination much to this point.

My brother had to go to work earlier than I, so it was just me at the track, under the watchful eye of Baldy.

In fact, Baldy got me a job with the feed man, Bill Rizzuto, so my entire life became the track. A lot of people became aware of who I was, the backstretch being like a small town. I can't say I got to know many of them. I didn't talk a lot in those days, and I've always been bad with names, of people anyway.

I knew the names of the horses at Officer's Citation's claiming level, and of the fillies at my claiming level, would be the best I could describe the way my brain was working that year. I came to learn the names of the best customers, and who employed the best looking grooms and gallop girls.

We settled into a routine. I would get to the track around seven in the morning, get a coffee to go, and toss Officer's Citation his breakfast, a full coffee can of oats. I would fill his water bucket and head back to the cafe to meet Baldy, slamming down breakfast if I had time, usually ten minutes.

Russ Janish, a crony of Baldy's, a good friend of the family, a former trainer, and a jock's agent observed that I was a good doer, a horse that stayed in the feed tub. It was true enough. I'd buy a racing form if the new edition was out, and wait for Baldy to arrive. Usually, he would be with my aunt Judy, but sometimes he would be alone.

Russ Janish was a mainstay in many of the stories I would hear about life at the track. The best times were those mornings when my brother and I would meet Marv and Baldy at the track. We'd all have coffee with Russ, and I don't remember a subject that didn't involve the racetrack in some way. I don't think I ever heard Marv say Reagan or Nixon at any racetrack we visited, now that I think about it.

One of those mornings, Marv shared some history about the friendship between the Putzier brothers and Russ. In 1969, Russ was training a horse, and they wound up racing against him. As Marv and Baldy studied the racing form, handicapping the race, Marv looked over at Baldy, and may have said something along the lines of, "Hell, why not kill the speed and bet on that shitter of Janish's?"

Killing the speed means forcing the pacesetter into a speed dual by running as fast as the horse could go early in the race, forcing the front runner to burn himself out trying to keep up, and setting the race up for the come from behinders, or closers, to win.

It isn't legal to bet on another horse in a race you are competing in, and I am not a first-hand witness, so I can't say for sure what happened. As the story went, however, the speed was in fact killed, and Russell's horse won. Russ didn't bet on his horse but was happy to get the win.

Russ was avoiding them a little but wasn't surprised when they congratulated him. After all, they were friends. He was a little surprised when they bought him breakfast, however, and how jovial they were, considering he had outrun them.

"It seemed like the least we could do," was all Marv would say about the breakfast, giving me a wink.

Russ came to believe they bet on his horse. "They bought me steak and eggs, for chrissakes." He still seemed a little indignant nearly twenty years after the fact. "Couldn't let a guy know?"

Another time they raced against each other, Russ's horse was running alongside another horse around the clubhouse turn, and then suddenly was pushed sideways, knocked off stride, eliminated from contention, and finished off the board. Russell was not happy.

The Putzier horse, a filly named "Who" won the race.

The next morning, after training hours, the replays of the previous day's races were shown over on the front side. Baldy and Russ walked over together to watch them, Russ wanting to see who wiped out his horse. Who was correct, as they were soon to discover.

Describing it, Baldy said, "As we watched the replay, I started to get a message. Who stuck a shoulder into that shitter a Janish's, damn near put her clear out in the middle of the track." Baldy said Russ was so mad, they didn't speak the entire walk back to the barn and for several days afterward.

"Who was a bulldog," Marv said. "Like to kill me when we were trying to break her. Her and that God damned Faydee."

"Those Double Reigh's were tough sonsabitches," Baldy said. "But they could run."

Barbara's Backstretch Cafe was a pretty cool place.

We'd walk slowly back to the stall, getting there as the renovation of the track started. The renovation consisted of two tractors, each pulling a harrow around the track. Quite a bit fancier harrow than I saw back on the farm, but still a harrow. This took about twenty minutes or so, and I used the time to tack up or groom and saddle the horse.

Around the barn, we called Officer's Citation Provy. Except for Baldy, who either referred to him as Officer's Citation, or any number of mildly profane descriptions accompanied by a gesture toward the horse with his good bad hand. "Hang that cheap son of a bitch on the walker," would be a generic example.

Baldy believed his name was his name, and his name was on the registration papers.

Marv believed they named themselves, eventually.

Officer's Citation came to be called Provy because there was another horse on the track by the same sire who was named Big Provolone. Officers Citation, a little horse for a Thoroughbred, then became Little Provolone, and soon Provy.

We had a horse in 1990 named Nan Sea's Flyer, who Marv called Willy Wedgehead.

"That one fits," Baldy said.

About the only other thing they disagreed on at the track besides Secretariat was race strategy, Marv preferring to be close to or on the lead, Baldy preferring to come from way off the pace. Baldy loved Secretariat, Marv thought he was overrated by people who never saw Citation run. Marv would cite the fact that trainer H. Allen Jerkins outran Secretariat with two different horses, Onion and Prove Out, neither of which could be considered great. Jerkins said of Secretariat, "He could be had if you caught him going the wrong way."

They are both lying in their graves now, Marv and Baldy, side by side, still disagreeing on whether or not to take back, or be on the engine. Probably arguing about Secretariat and agreeing about Swaps.

1987 was a great year in horse racing, and 1989 brought us a rivalry between Easy Goer and Sunday Silence that recalled fond memories of Affirmed and Alydar in 1978. But I found myself fascinated by stories of the great horses of yesteryear, the horses of the fifties and the sixties when horse racing and my parents were in their prime. Horses named Swaps, Ribot, Nashua, Northern Dancer, Damascus, and Dr. Fager, who holds a world record that still stands today, 1:32:1/5 for one mile.

The gallop boy, Leonard, would show up at the barn sometime during the renovation, usually with five or ten minutes to spare. He was soft spoken and was about halfway between my age and Baldy's. He was easy to get along with and would inspect the saddle as he was ready to be legged up, lifted by the foot up on to the back of the horse. He tacked about a hundred and forty-five pounds, I would estimate.

31

The racetrack is the only place in the world I know of where you can ask a woman how much she weighs without getting punched. If you get used to legging up a hundred and fifty-pound gallop boy, you can almost throw a hundred and twenty-pound jockey over the horse on race day if you aren't paying attention.

So I would leg him up, and begin to lead the horse to the track, being careful to come straight out the stall door and be in the center of the opening. I usually came out backward in front of the horse, alert in case he was to lunge forward. You had to stay alert around these Thoroughbreds.

Leonard would reach down and tighten the girth by pulling up on two leather straps under the saddle skirt, pointing his knee outward as he did so. He did this on both sides of the saddle, the girth being padded leather with elastic on the end, attached to a leather strap on the saddle by a buckle on the girth.

He would have adjusted the stirrup length while he was on the ground, the shorter the stirrup, the more leverage for the rider. Leonard kept them medium length, knowing the horse would pull hard when galloping slow but would go slow if he was made to. We put the rings on, one rein running through each ring, attached to the girth with a strap that ran between the horse's front legs. This kept his head down and made him easier to control. If the horse reared up on his hind legs while wearing the rings, he could flip over backward.

There were a lot of ways to cripple yourself on the track. You had to respect what the exercise riders and jockeys went through for the sport they loved. Underpaid and underinsured, usually.

As Leonard would finish his adjustments, he would say to me, "I've got him," the signal to let go of the rein and step to the side. Baldy and I would follow Leonard and the horse to the gap, and find ourselves a spot by the rail.

Leonard would go through the gap onto the track, and we would see him again as he rode the horse along the inside of the outside rail, going opposite the way the horses galloped, backtracking. He would backtrack the horse about an eighth of a mile at a walk, up to where the four-furlong and mile and an eighth races started, the half-mile chute.

He would turn the horse to the right and stop, letting the horse take in his surroundings. Then Leonard would urge Officer's Citation into a walk, then a slow trot, and usually into a slow gallop within a few strides. He would gallop toward the outside of the track with the slow gallopers, the medium gallopers a little further inside, the two-minute lickers and fast gallopers inside them, and the rail was reserved for the workers, the horses undergoing timed workouts.

We were close to the track, so there wouldn't be much traffic as Officer's Citation made his way down the length of the backstretch the first time. As the horses from the barns further away began to enter the track, our view would be interrupted by the horses backtracking. Some of them would be jogging, some walking, and signs were posted admonishing the riders, "No jogging or galloping wrong way of track".

The rail next to the guinea stand would become crowded as owners, trainers and grooms settled in to watch their horses, still optimistic in the early spring.

The guinea stand itself would become a beehive of activity, providing a slightly better view for those who chose to watch from inside. On top, about twenty feet high, was the clockers tower, from which the workouts were timed. I was a month away from timed workouts with my horse, according to my uncle and mentor at the track. "If we can hold the son of a bitch together," Baldy said.

The slow gallop was a big part of holding him together. I would watch as he galloped into the far turn, his head bowed as he strained against the hold Leonard had on him, well into the bit. I would see a white foam between his legs as he began to perspire, getting his work in with the other horses, slowly galloping himself into shape.

Leonard would gather up the reins, one on top of the other, locking them together with his fingers. This was known as throwing a cross. Throwing a short cross meant taking a strong hold on the horse, restraining him as much as possible. Officer's Citation was a well-schooled professional, but he was a horse who felt good. On the track and wanting to run he took a good hold of the bit and got a lot out of his slow gallops.

I couldn't see him that well across the track as he made his way past the grandstand, and the view was obstructed by the back of the tote board, the digital display that gave the odds and results when the horses were racing. I would watch for him to come into view as he entered the clubhouse turn, just past the finish line. I could listen to the trainers and grooms talking, some joking, all happy to be at the races even if they didn't all show it.

Officer's Citation would come back into view, still with his head bowed, slowly and rhythmically galloping his way toward us now, into the backstretch for the second time. You could hear him snorting as he galloped, sounding like a sort of steam engine, chugging slowly down the track. I would inspect him closely as he galloped by, just watching him as a horse, admiring him, but not understanding yet what it was to be transfixed by these horses.

Thoroughbreds were about to become my religion, but I hadn't seen the light yet.

I didn't really even know what I was looking at when I inspected him as he went by. He was a nice looking horse, but I couldn't speak intelligently about conformation. Growing up in the farm country, if we learned about conformation, it was the conformation of a meat producing animal, and not a horse. I could say a horse looked good, but I couldn't tell you exactly why it looked good.

He went around the track again, pulled up just before the far turn, on the north end of the track, and came walking up along the outside rail, backtracking to the gap. This was our sixth gallop, and I watched as Leonard turned him to the right. Officer's Citation pricked his ears and watched as a horse went galloping buy, running into a quarter mile work. I was beginning to notice how picturesque the Thoroughbred was, silhouetted against the beautiful infield at Playfair Race Course.

Leonard patted him on the shoulder, rubbed his mane a little, and turned him back to the left. They went off the track, coming around the north end of the barrier fence in front of the gap. The barrier was designed to look like a continuous fence to the nearsighted Thoroughbreds as they galloped on the track.

Baldy and I walked back to the stall, Baldy sitting on a straw bale in front of the stall as I met Leonard coming back from the track. Leonard ducked as he rode into the stall, turned the horse and dismounted smoothly, barely making a noise as his feet hit the ground.

"OK?" he asked, as I held the reins and he unbuckled the girth and removed the saddle, careful to disconnect the rings from the girth without spooking the horse.

"Ok".

Leonard said to Baldy, "Tomorrow?"

"Let's give him a day off," Baldy replied.

"See you Monday," said Leonard, and headed to his next barn.

I held Officer's Citation's halter with my right arm over his neck and removed his bridle with my left. Setting the bridle in his feed tub, I put his halter on, gave him a small drink of water, and led him to the hot walker, angling up to the walker as it was turning, merging in and attaching the bungee to his halter on the inside ring, so he had as much freedom of movement as possible. I stepped to the inside, gave him a pat on the rump and exited the hot walker between him and the horse on the arm behind him.

"That's a good way to get kicked, Bass," said Baldy as he watched all this. Everything was okay, except for the pat on the hindquarters.

I headed for the feed room to get the wheelbarrow and pitchfork, so I could clean his stall while he cooled out. In those days we still bedded with straw, and I separated the dirty from the reusable, taking a load or two out to the cart, pulling the reusable straw to the middle, and shaking out the new straw around the outside, leveling it all with a pitchfork, the straw about six inches deep.

I rinsed the water bucket, refilled it and hung it on the wall, filled up his hay net, and walked out to see if he was ready to come in.

"Bass," said Baldy, " gimme a smoke."

I learned a lot on smoke breaks with Baldy.

We'd move away from the barn, away from the combustibles, and Baldy would smoke and point out things like a short-stepping horse, maybe indicating a problem. He could usually tell you the problem, but it was difficult to pick up the nuance for me. I was learning to look and listen.

I took the shank, a leather strap about an inch wide and quarter inch thick, six feet long with a twenty inch braided chain at the end with a snap on it, and attached it to Officer's Citation's halter as he walked. I unhooked him from the walker as it turned, and led him to his stall as the walker's arm came around to the front of the walking ring.

It was usually about 9:30 when we finished, and I would walk with Baldy back to the cafe. We would have a coffee and study our racing forms before I had to go to work when the barn area opened for traffic at ten. Only then could I begin making my feed deliveries.

Life at the track is a pretty good life, and I was enjoying it quite a bit. I already couldn't understand why anyone would want to do anything else.

The Program

His name was Marvin Putzier, Jr, and at the time, he went by the nickname of Deke. I can tell you the back story of his nickname, it was after the astronaut Deke Slayton. The space program must have stirred my mother's imagination, as I was named after a fighter pilot named Colin Kelly, at least that is what she told me. I came to believe something different, but we will get to that.

Deke was a year and a few months older than I, and frankly, a better hand with the horses. He would help my dad break colts, Marv on the big Quarter Horse, "snubbing" or leading Deke on a two or three-year-old colt with a short, heavy lead rope wrapped around the saddle horn. This was so the colt couldn't buck. They could keep the colt in motion, teaching and schooling the colt, getting him used to good habits, and preparing him for a smooth transition into being able to go for a solo ride.

The horse used to lead another is known as a pony horse at the track. I've seen them called a comfort horse in books and magazines, but I have never heard this term on the backstretch.

Sometimes, if the colt was going well and moving freely, Marv would reach down and unsnap the rope from the colt, and Deke would be riding solo in the round pen. It usually went pretty well. If you don't allow them to develop bad habits, you can break a young horse fairly quickly.

We would buy horses around the county and fatten them up for thirty or forty-five days, and sell them at the auction. Usually, this was at Stockland Livestock Exchange in Spokane, located on Freya street, not far from Playfair. We hit all the auctions in eastern Washington state at one time or another. Wherever horses were bought and sold was usually where you would find us on Saturday.

Stockland and Playfair, as well as the Stockyards Inn, just around the corner from Stockland, no longer exist. The racetrack and the auction have been razed and resurrected as industrial parks. The Stockyards Inn, a restaurant, lounge, card room, and nightclub frequented by racetrackers and stockmen and women, changed names and now appears to be closed. It is like the street corner of my youth and young adulthood never existed, except in my mind.

You will get to know the Stockyards Inn, believe me.

We would take these skinny or otherwise new to us horses, and ride them, Deke and Dad on the tough ones, me on the older horses who were, as Marv put it, 'spoiled'. These were horses whose owners and riders were overmatched or mismatched. Many of these horses were used to getting their way with their riders, had fallen into bad habits, and had forgotten who was supposed to be the boss.

These bad habits and headstrong horses changed their way of thinking abruptly, usually not long after backing out of the pickup truck Marv drove. We would unload them onto the dirt bank we used for a loading chute, the bank being about the same height of the truck bed with the tailgate down.

We spent many evenings and weekends 'unspoiling' horses and ponies, often riding across the fallowed wheat fields which surrounded the small town we grew up in until 1978, Endicott Washington. Marv would smack the horse Deke or I were riding on the ass, let out a whoop, and suddenly we would be racing toward an unknown finish line, riding to ride and running to run.

I had at least a ten-pound weight allowance back then. Caution always went out the window, and we were all in to the finish line. These horses were all new to us, so we didn't know who could run until after the race. We all won a few, anyway. We would ride some tired and well-mannered horses back home, often working in the barn until after dark cleaning the stalls and bedding the horses down.

We would mix up about four gallons of grain for each horse,

two gallons and a half of oats, a gallon of "sweet feed", a mixture of oats, barley, corn, and molasses, then add an additional quart or so of cracked corn. We would then add various pelletized, powdered, and liquid vitamins and supplements, mixed together with a pretty good pinch of salt. "Rolling it to them," Marv would say.

Any vet in the world would say we fed too much, and any one of them would also tell us that our horses were in great condition. We continued to do it wrong, as the results spoke for themselves. Marv was a horseman, anyone who knew him would tell you so. It was his feeding program, and Baldy concurred completely.

Marv built a nice set of plywood stock racks for his Ford pick-up truck. Five pieces of plywood, two sides, a front, and two doors. We would drop the sides on, three two by two legs extending about 4 inches below the plywood which fit into the holes in the top of the side of the truck bed wall.

We would then take a steel rod, slightly wider than the truck bed, a half inch in diameter and threaded on one end, a nut and washer welded on the other, and slide it through one rack, across and through the other side. We would then attach a washer and nut on the outside of the plywood, drop the front in, and tighten the nut until the racks were fitted snugly in place.

The two doors we attached by dropping pins through the hinges on the doors, and they would be held closed by a hasp, and the final pieces were a piece of rubber covered plywood on the floor, with three one by four boards nailed to the floor so that if the horse slipped, he wouldn't go all the way down, and four rubber mats to cover any exposed metal on the floor. Finally, a three-inch-wide piece of flat steel with slots on each end was snapped into place as a safety precaution against the back doors getting kicked open.

Simple, right?

My brother and I never got through the job of putting these racks on without getting into a fist fight, never, not once. I think after the first five times, we sort of felt obligated to continue fighting, tradition being what it is. Men and boys who have brothers understand this.

We had a good relationship as kids, did just about everything together. Deke was better with the horses atop their back, and around the barn. There were horses he could connect with that I couldn't, and vice-versa. He was built like a wide receiver, tall and slender, and I was built like a linebacker, always a couple of inches shorter and a few pounds heavier than he, even to this day. He ended up over six feet tall, I topped out at seventeen one hands tall, same as Marv.

In our late teens, I could buy beer and get into bars, and Deke was asked for ID until he was nearly thirty. It was funny then, not so much now. We won a ton of bets when people would try to guess who was older.

We used to wait all day for Sunday when we were kids, so we could watch football. But then we always ended up out in the yard playing football ourselves, one on one. Deke, being the oldest, of course, made the rules, and decreed that the rule was, 'all passing', meaning that we had to throw the ball higher than our heads, pass it to ourselves, or it didn't count. Naturally, this gave the advantage to the tall guy. Pretty much why he learned to catch, and I learned to tackle. I threw a few interceptions in those days, let me tell you.

I usually did a better job of cleaning stalls, fixing fences and had a much bigger fear of my father's reprisals than Deke ever did. Marv never raised a hand to us, never whipped, or beat us. We had no doubt, however, that there were lines not to be crossed.

Marv was a boxer in the navy, and a good one, knocking out a gold glove finalist in the first round. His hands were lightning quick, and he moved like a cat. He was pretty solid, not much fat, stayed active working construction and shoeing horses. More than anything, he taught us to think for ourselves and to not be afraid to be unconventional in our methods.

Deke knew instinctively what Marv was thinking all the time, while I was usually either lost in the fog or not paying attention at all. What I paid attention to were the rations of grain each horse got, the amounts of vitamins and supplements to give, who got an extra scoop of corn to put the fat on, who got red cell, and iron supplement that had an indescribable smell that reminds me of the racetrack, and who didn't.

I was usually raising a hog to take to the livestock shows, but Deke never did. Dogs and I always got along. We had paper routes, and I would play with one of the dogs on the route, next to a sign that said 'Beware of Dog'. We were a week into this ritual before I ever saw the sign.

Long story short, when it came to the horses, Deke was Marv's first choice, and it wasn't a bad choice. Most other animals, I probably got along with a little better.

But then fate, or maybe favoritism, intervened for me at the track.

Baldy arranged for Leonard to come to the barn to gallop after Deke had to go to work, and it pissed Deke off. He said twice, "I can't be here then." Baldy ignored him.

By default, I got the job.

One of those early spring mornings we were there, Baldy

and I, Officers Citation tacked up and waiting for Leonard. We were about six weeks into training now, two weeks with a pony, and four weeks worth of slow gallops, either five or six days a week, with one or two days off, depending.

"It's tough to keep your horse in the stall when everyone else is taking theirs to the track," Baldy said, "but it's never the wrong choice."

In the mornings, early, the first thing I would do after arriving at the barn was to run my hands over Officer's Citation's legs, checking for heat. The skin and bones of the horse would be cold, and heat is the sign of inflammation. Sometimes it was faint, and so I had to trust what my fingers were feeling.

To this point, Officer's Citation was staying cold as ice. "Keep an eye on that left knee," Baldy said to me.

The bones on a horse correspond with the bones of a human, the front legs on a horse matching those of the human arm. The elbow is where you might think the armpit of a horse would be. The knee on a horse would correspond to the wrist on a human, the shin bone the hand, the knuckle as the ankle, and the bones which correspond with fingers fused together to form the foundation of the hoof.

The hoof is consistent, more or less, to the texture of the human finger and toenails, and if you don't have healthy feet, you don't have a horse, much less a racehorse. In the mornings before I put the tack on, I would clean his feet, picking the compacted dirt out of his feet with a hoof pick, a small tool that fits in your back pocket and abused your car seat when you forgot it was in your pocket. We had several hoof picks, and when we ran out, I would often find them in my vehicle. Growing up, hoof picks tended to collect on a small table by the back door, and Marv's coffee cups tended to decorate the tops of the fence posts.

Once a week, a little more often if necessary, I would apply something called 'Hooflex' to the feet. Hooflex is a mixture of turpentine and other petroleum distillates and forms a shellac-like substance, sticky and gooey, with a brush attached to the lid. The turpentine penetrates into the hoof, and from the inside out, it hardens the hoof in some manner. When shellac dries it is much like super durable nail polish.

Some hoof treatments were lanolin, and I used them a few days after the Hooflex to keep the hoof firm yet pliable. The lanolin provided the added benefit creating a no-stick surface on the hoof, so the hoof would shed the dirt easily as the horse was running.

The farriers always said we had a good program, and we did. W took care of the horse from the feet up. Officer's Citation was good about not abusing me when I was holding his back leg over my knee, either extending backward or forward, depending if I was working on the hoof wall or the bottom of his foot.

I have seen trainers spray the bottom of a horse's feet with Teflon cooking spray before a race, but lanolin and even hooflex always worked well enough for us. Spraying a Thoroughbred's feet with an aerosol can is a great way to get your head kicked off.

The program didn't change but slightly when we were about to start revving him up with timed workouts. In 1987, you needed three certified works at distances not less than three furlongs, or three-eighths of a mile, faster than a certain time, to qualify to race.

Two-year-olds had to work fast, until they learned why they were at the track. Some two-year-olds take a lot of time. If you put blinkers on a two-year-old, they will get into the bit faster.

But some instinctively know what they were born to do, and naturally get into the bit very quickly, always pulling against the rider, showing a willingness and eagerness to run. Baldy never put blinkers on any horse if he could help it, and never two-year-olds. Baldy always played the long game.

Older horses who had been through the gate, or had run a few races, didn't need fast works. They loved to run fast if you had their head right and were mentally in a good frame of mind. You had to restrain them, and you had to be careful not to ever let them get the advantage if you were riding. If a Thoroughbred is going to run off with his rider, he is going to run off, there is little you can do. You can prevent this by using the rings, which provide extra leverage. When we were ready for a timed workout, we would go to the track without rings.

We were still about a month away, however, from his first official work.

For four days, we slow galloped, same as always.

The fifth day, Baldy said to Leonard, "Go ahead and let him run a little down the lane." Baldy wanted the horse to stretch his legs out, and do an easy wind sprint in the home stretch, from the eighth pole to the wire.

So it was still the same, without rings, for the first lap around the track. Leonard was patient, and at the three-sixteenths pole, he threw a slightly longer cross, letting the reins out a notch. There is a pole every sixteenth of a mile from the wire, all the way around the track, letting the jockeys know how far they are from home. Sixteenth markers are always black, eighths are green, quarters and half are red.

Officer's Citation, understanding his cue, began to accelerate a little, Leonard not giving him too much rein. As they approached the eighth pole, he let out another notch, and

Officer's Citation, still with his head bowed, still straining, accelerated some more, approaching the pace of a two-minute lick. This was all Leonard allowed as they went under the wire. Leonard let the horse gallop out freely but slowly, pulling him up in the normal spot, about twenty yards past the gap at the beginning of the far turn.

Baldy slapped the top of the outside rail, nodded his head and said, "Good," as we watched the horse pull up.

They backtracked to the gap, and as they turned to face the track, Officer's Citation was a little less willing to stop and stand still, but Leonard, the hand that he was, soon had him relaxed and stopped. Officer's Citation appeared to take a deep breath, let it out, and then turned to come off the track. He was a bouncier horse coming back to the barn.

The main difference at the barn, I gave him a bath at the wash rack. He wasn't breathing very hard, but Baldy admonished me to not let him drink too much. I had a bucket filled with warm water, and a large sponge, and washed him much like you would a car, soaping with the sponge, rinsing with a moderate flow of water from the hose, making sure to get the sand from between his hind legs, and everywhere else. I was also about to get a basic lesson in cooling out a hot horse, even if he wasn't that hot.

If a hot horse drinks too much, they can get stomach cramps, and sometimes 'tie up', or suffer from muscle spasms.

I gave him about two swallows before and after his bath, holding the water bucket up to him. Then I put the bucket down and put my horse on the hotwalker. About every five minutes or so, I would stop the walker and give him a small drink, doing this until he stopped drinking, or was 'watered out'. He took about three drinks. A little more time on the walker and he was cool and dry. I thought I was beginning to see a little more definition in his muscles.

The cooling out process usually took about a half hour, watering out after a work or race about twenty minutes. This usually gave me ten minutes or so just to watch the horse on the walker, sometimes with Baldy, and sometimes not. Hours I would spend watching Officer's Citation on the walker that year, and none of those hours were wasted.

Our first two phases of training at the track were over, and it was time to start mapping out a schedule for the timed workouts.

Time Drills

Citation galloping at Santa Anita

We gave Officer's Citation two days off and would have given him three, but he was demanding to go back to the track. He was a kind little horse, but he could kick the hell out of a stall if he was rested too long. He was a tougher horse to handle around the barn after having been allowed to stretch his legs. He knew why he was here, and he was where he wanted to be. Mentally, he was right.

Physically, the signs you watch for are mostly in the morning. He cleaned up his feed, and that was the best indication that we were good to go. His legs were still ice cold. So far, so good. As far as I knew, it always went like clockwork.

"Starting to come up on his toes," Marv said.

"Might take some work to keep this son of a bitch cooled out," was Baldy's reply.

It wasn't the worst problem to have. If run is on their mind, training will progress rapidly . But we were a long ways from a race, and it was crucial to keep the horse relaxed.

For a while, this is how the routine went. Slow gallop four days, and then let him run a little on the fifth day, at gradually increased distances. We worked up gradually, a sixteenth at a time, until finally, after about four weeks, we were ready for our first timed workout, going three furlongs.

Both racing and timed workouts, the benchmark is generally twelve seconds for each eighth of a mile. Times clocked in less than twelve seconds per eighth are generally considered fast fractions, and of course, slower is slow. Times are measured in full seconds and fifths of a second, one-fifth of a second generally considered one length on the track.

If the winning horse in a four-furlong race was timed in forty-eight seconds flat, and the second place horse was one length behind, his time would be forty-eight and one-fifth of a second, or forty-eight and one.

So we worked Officer's Citation three-eighths of a mile, and Leonard let him roll into it. Leonard let out a notch on the reins at about the seven-sixteenths pole at the head of the backstretch, so we had a good view as the horse was getting into stride. Leonard kept a good hold on him, and Officer's Citation was pulling against the bit, his head bowed, straining against Leonard and a short cross. He went evenly and galloped out easily, pulling up after the work when he was nearly back into the homestretch.

Baldy looked up to the clocker's tower and asked, "What did you catch Officer's Citation in?"

"Thirty-nine and two" came back the reply.

Baldy smacked the rail with his hand, and said, "good." A nice slow work, and a sound horse coming back to the barn.

Officer's Citation practically skipped back to the barn, his aluminum shoes clacking out a tap-dance rhythm on the pavement. He was no longer a gentle and well-mannered horse. Not mean, but on the muscle. It was becoming a little more work and a lot more fun. We went through the routine one more time, washing him, hanging him on the walker, cooling him out.

I used this time to strip all the old straw from his stall and bed it down with an entire bale of fresh straw. I filled his hay net and water bucket, and as I was done with this about ten minutes before he was ready to come in, I had time to admire my horse on the walker. He was showing more definition in his muscles, and his veins tended to become more pronounced against his skin after exerting himself. He was sleek and beautiful, shining in the morning sun. His head was up and he was energetic on the walker, his ears pricked forward.

The work hadn't appeared to take much out of him. We would know for sure tomorrow morning.

We had some time and went and had breakfast at the cafe. We weren't going off track much anymore since this was where

I worked. Anytime it was my choice, we went to Barbara's Backstretch Cafe. It wasn't just for the food, but for the people and the atmosphere. I didn't know it yet, but I was already forming an addiction to the life.

"Cut him back about half a can when you feed tonight, Bass," said Baldy, as we ate breakfast. "Want to make sure he cleans up."

The next morning, I arrived around seven, an hour before it was necessary. I liked to be able to go to the rail and see the horses on the track in the mornings. This particular morning, I wanted to see how the horse pulled up.

I turned the corner to the barn and there he was, his head out of the stall, his ears pricked forward, his intelligent eyes looking toward me. He looked great, but something wasn't right. As I walked toward him, something about the whole picture was off, and I couldn't quite put it together.

I touched the bottom stall chain, and the top chain fell to the ground. First one side and then the other, and finally the spring mechanism fell out of the snap. These were two thoroughly broken snaps I was looking at. Just then, the neighboring trainer, Bob, came out of his tack room.

"Hey, your horse had his top chain down when I got here."

I felt the same sensation as when you first see the blue lights in the rearview mirror.

"Was he out?"

"No, he settled for breaking the snap. I don't think he was out."

"Thanks, Bob." That was a relief, the fact that Officer's Citation didn't get out of his stall and hurt himself.

Bob was the sort of guy reminded you of the poker player who fumbles and lucks his way into taking all the money home at the end of the night. He outran more than one trainer who probably thought he was a fool.

"Old Bob's gonna school a few people if his horses run as good as they look," Marv remarked the weekend after Bob moved in. Bob did school a few people. He ran his horses at the level where they could win and he even stole a few purses at long odds in feature races. Bob didn't gamble, but I bet enough on his horses for both of us. He was a good neighbor to have, looked out for us, and tended to his own business. He said to me once, "I'm not broke, but I got a twenty dollar bill I been taking pretty good care of for a couple of days." I knew what he meant.

At about this time we started a little tradition, due to a trend the guy who ran a small retail tack shop at the track noticed after a couple of weeks. About the time our third timed work was scheduled, he would throw a handful of brass snaps on the counter every time I went to the tack shop, whether I asked or not. I don't remember ever knowing his name, but he was the first person on the Officer's Citation bandwagon. "I love that horse of yours, he buys a half dozen snaps a week," he said.

I went over the horse, and everything looked fine. He wasn't sweating, had cleaned up his feed and eaten most of his hay. He just felt good, and when he did, he would occasionally break from the starting gate in his own stall and stress test the top snaps.

I didn't want to close the bottom door on the stall, so I eventually began putting two snaps on each end. Zinc would break, brass would bend. The test limit was apparently a nine hundred pound Thoroughbred with ice-cold legs.

But on the track, we weren't trying to see how fast he was, we were working him into shape. His works would be considered slow, none of the three-furlong works being faster than about thirty-eight seconds, all of them designated as breezing, a term meaning not fully extended, or all out. If a workout was termed handily, it meant that the horse was close to running as fast as he could. Work times were generally slower than race times by a couple of seconds. One minute twelve seconds for six furlongs would be a very fast work, but a slow race. Competition is the only explanation I can offer for the difference in times..

The Putzier Brothers preferred slow works for one particular reason, and that reason was to bring a sound horse back to the barn every time we took him to the track. The fastest workout of the day at the distance is referred to as a 'bullet' work, and you don't win anything for a bullet work.

The spring progressed, and as we moved into June, the horse was getting fit. Aside from an occasional warm ankle or shin, we didn't miss much training. We never trained on a wet track, so rain was an automatic day off.

There was a day when Leonard wasn't there, and we wanted to get the horse out. It was a weekend because Marv and Deke were there.

Baldy and I were sitting at the gap, waiting for the particular rider we wanted to come by since they all had to come to the gap sooner or later anyway. Marv and Deke, however, preferred to stay in motion, and went looking for the rider, each covering a different portion of the backstretch.

I sat with Baldy on the bench at the gap, and it was a perfect spring day. I never knew what Baldy might say, or who might come by to say hi. I took many quizzes on this bench, on days just like this. I'm sure we were laughing about something, or at someone. I was lighting cigarettes for Baldy, and learning from him.

Marv came hustling by, hardly breaking stride, walking north to south, and said, "You see him?' Marv was walking fast, headed south as Baldy and I indicated we had not seen the rider. About a minute later, Deke came by, walking south to north and said, "Seen him?" Deke, never breaking stride and continuing north, hardly acknowledged the negative reply. Baldy looked after Deke for a contemplative moment. "Y'know Bass," he said, "they'd have fucked up bad had they named you Marvin junior, and not him."

It kind of made me think, but it also made me laugh out loud. I lit a cigarette for Baldy and knew I had just gained a life-long memory. I told Carol, my mother, about it, and we both had a pretty good laugh. It was a correct assessment, just never before put so eloquently.

It wasn't just Marv and Baldy, Carol was pretty sharp herself, and enjoyed humor as much as the rest of us.

Years later, she and I were in the paddock at Emerald Downs, watching Deke, now going by Marvin Jr, saddle a horse he was training for a lawyer friend of his. At Emerald, there is a covered saddling enclosure with a walking ring round it, and another ring outside where the owners and other connections could be in the paddock. It was where the trainers legged up the jockeys before the race. It was where everyone got introduced to whatever family members were involved.

Someone connected to the horse approached us and said, "We've been praying for you all day. Good luck!"

"Thank you," I replied. "He looks good."

As we walked out to the rail, Carol said to me, "What do you think Colin, should we pray?"

Having given the subject a fair amount of thought over the years, I said, "I'm not sure He would approve of us being at the racetrack in the first place, to tell you the truth."

"Well I hope she at least puts in a good word for the horse," carol replied, laughing.

"You can still pray," I said.

"No," she said, looking at the tote board, pretty serious when it came to her gambling. Not wanting to take any chances, she said, "I'm afraid you might be right."

Marv's client, Tom, who was a lawyer, was walking beside me as I led his horse, Erikstratton, to the paddock to be saddled for a race he would win, his maiden victory.

Tom asked, "whaddya think, Cole, is he gonna win?"

"If one of you lawyers don't run up and settle for third before the race, yeah, we should be alright," I answered.

"Why you gotta be a hater?" he said.

Because I had recently been introduced to the pleasures of the civil court, is why. I had fifty thousand reasons, but I didn't answer. Tom already knew.

I think Deke might have had a heart attack if he knew I was talking to his client that way. But Tom was a special case, and we had a pretty good relationship. He told me once, "It was so cold in Bellingham this morning, I had my hands in my own pockets." It had to be cold if a lawyer had his hands in his own pockets.

Anyway, all of that was twenty years in the future.

For now, it was June and we were getting closer. We were stretching Officer's Citation out. His next work would be at the distance of four furlongs, one-half mile. Then, if everything stayed on schedule, we would work him around both turns, five furlongs. If that went well, we would be ready for a race. We were about three weeks away, his first race in 1987 coming up on July 5th.

These next few weeks would end up leaving me with a few significant impressions.

Hustling Book

Ribot

Monday, June 15, 1987, was no more significant than the previous Mondays, except we were two works from a race. We had given the horse two days off, so instead of going straight to the barn when I got to the track I went to the tack shop to buy some new snaps. I also bought a hoof pick, because you couldn't have too many of either. I don't think we ever actually lost a hoof pick, but it didn't hurt to have one for each pocket and each vehicle.

I took the items to the barn and gave Officer's Citation his can of oats, rinsed and filled his water bucket and did a few stall repairs while he was eating. I may not have said two words to people at the track all morning, but I promise you, I talked to the horse all the way through breakfast. He was a good listener and didn't seem to be very critical of any of my ideas.

"How's that look, kiddo?" I said to him as I finished repairing the chains.

He never replied. He didn't look very impressed. We would find out soon enough.

I finished my early chores, then walked to the cafe and got a half order of the Backstretch Scramble and waited for Baldy to arrive.

This was usually when I would run into the friends and associates who had known Marv and Baldy for years, and where I would listen to stories about my father and uncle, usually the ones they weren't as willing to tell. I loved having breakfast at Barbara's Backstretch Cafe.

Marv and Baldy were very respected horsemen, but the majority of their buddies wouldn't say much more than hello to me at first. Once they had confirmed that I showed up on time, and showed up every day, they were a little more willing to accept me at the table.

The racetrack is the only place where I was ever concerned about what people thought of me. To earn the respect of a good horseman is what it means to me to earn respect.

Besides that, I always enjoyed listening to them talk to each other. I liked how some were always jovial, and some were always sour. Some of them were hot one day and cold the next, some were rich, some were poor, and all had repeatedly learned the most common lesson taught at the racetrack, the lesson of humility.

I hadn't learned much humility yet, but at this point I hadn't learned to be arrogant, so the humility lesson wasn't necessary. When it did come, it wasn't a very hard lesson the first couple of times, but it was disappointing.

I've often heard people receiving awards describe the experience as 'humbling'. This has not been my experience. Any awards I've ever received were far more rewarding than humbling.

A humbling experience is leading the even-money favorite to the saddling ring, and then leading the well-beaten seventh-place finisher back to the barn. That is not quite the same feeling as receiving an award. You learn not to brag about your horse. Or even your car, for that matter. You try to learn to not be too disappointed with running second.

Whatever lessons I had learned so far at the track, I was still unaware of. Most of what I had learned seemed pretty simple so far, a bunch of little things, nothing very big. It took quite a few more years for me to realize the little things are the big things in life, and at the track.

My mentors were not keeping it simple for me, they were teaching me to keep it simple. It was pretty much what we did with the saddle horses at home, only with aluminum racing plates and a leather shank instead of steel horseshoes and a cotton lead rope.

Baldy usually would arrive around eight, about the time I was done destroying the mound of deliciously unhealthy breakfast food disguised as a half-order. I would get us each a coffee to go, and I would walk beside him as he staggered to the barn. I don't remember ever not smiling or laughing during our walks to the barn. If a horse with a woman exercise rider walked by, he would raise his voice and say, "Loose horse." He was usually rewarded with a laugh or a dirty look, depending on how well they knew him. Such was the racetrack in 1987.

Baldy would walk up to the stall, the horse would walk up to him, and Baldy would smack the horse in the chest with the back of his best bad hand. Never once did this not occur. Stagger, stagger, clip, clop, smack. Like clockwork. "How the legs?" he usually asked.

"Cold."

"Well, tack the son of a bitch up in case the gallop boy shows."

The gallop boy always showed. By this time in the program, I would leg Leonard up in the stall and he would ride the horse out, turn left, and adjust the irons and tighten the girth as they made their way toward the gap. Once they were on the track, Leonard would backtrack at a walk for about thirty yards, and then ease him into a trot. Sometimes he would backtrack to the finish line before easing Officer's Citation into his slow gallop.

Even from the beginning, I always loved this part of the ritual. You had time to listen to the horseman and their cynical truisms. Horses would be continually arriving, backtracking past our spot on the rail, the trainers, owners, and grooms always making room for us. I once observed to Baldy that he must be well respected for that to happen, and his response was, "No, it's because I'm badly crippled, not well respected."

I asked Russ Janish if Baldy was well respected. "You ever hear how he got the name Baldy?" Russ asked me.

"Uh-uh," I said. Russ told me, and my innocence was gone forever. He didn't tell me the story, just what it was short for. It is difficult to imagine, but even more difficult to stop wondering about once you start.

"Hell no, he's not respected," Russ said, giving me a wink.

"Get the fuck out of here Janish, I'm trying to train a racehorse," Baldy said.

"I'll go find one for you," Russ said, insulting my horse as he went on his way, making his rounds as a jockeys agent, hustling book. Agenting was a good way to hang around the racetrack and make money doing it, provided you had a good rider. Russ had one, and Russ was the only person who knew it so far. He hustled off to get the word out.

A jockey's agent visits the trainers and represents certain jockeys. The agent will book rides for the jockey with the trainers, giving them first, or second call, or even third call in rare cases. They call this hustling book. First call means, if the horse the jockey is committed to runs in the race he entered, the jockey is committed to ride the horse, and the horse he had second call on will be ridden by another rider.

The race could only have as many horses as the starting gate could hold. In the case of Playfair, that number was ten. In those days, you didn't have to name a rider until the day before the race, when the programs were printed. You wanted to have a rider lined up at the draw, however. This wasn't as simple as getting a rider to commit and being done with it. The reason why was called an agent.

If fourteen horses entered a race, four of them would end up on what was called the "also eligible" list. These horses would be guaranteed to start in the next race they entered, unless one of the horses eligible to enter the starting gate withdrew from the race. When a horse in the gate scratched out of the race, the first horse on the also-eligible list would draw into the race and start from the ten hole. The post positions were determined by a blind draw in the racing office.

At the draw, you would learn the post position of your horse and whether or not your agent had an honest bone in his entire damned body. This was because an unscrupulous agent, which my training and experience have led me to believe is all of them, is not above verbally committing to first call on two, three, or even five horses. One horse and trainer get the jockey, and the others get "spun."

Baldy, in his younger days, had hustled some book and told me he once had seven first calls in one race. "I was hustling book for Dick Wright," he said, "So I had the best rider. I spun some of those poor bastards ten times that year. One of 'em hollered 'Ya son of a bitch, you fucked me again' right there at the draw."

An agent can get suspended for this kind of behavior, but you'd have to start shooting them to actually solve the problem. Or get a call slip, which is a commitment in writing. You always see agents with a pen in their hands, except when it is time to sign the call slip.

Once in a while, a guy named Keith Davis would hustle by. You could fill up a library with Keith Davis stories, and only about half of them would be lies. Probably not the ones you might think. Keith died a few years ago, and the backstretch has been a quieter and less interesting place ever since.

"Hey Clay, when you gonna run that cheap son of a bitch?" Keith hollered at me. It was probably ten years before he realized my name was Cole and not Clay.

Keith was loud and didn't hear very well. He was somewhere

around forty years old in 1987, was a jockey when he was younger, and now trained anywhere between two and five horses at any given time. He was also reliably profane, and a good horseman. He usually cracked the seal on his first beer at ten o'clock when the track closed for training. He was usually pretty drunk by afternoon feed time, but since he was just as loud and obnoxious when he was sober, no one seemed to mind.

Whenever I brought a date or a girlfriend to the track, not only did she have to meet the parents and extended family, she had to pass the acid test that was Keith Davis. I always tried to make her understand that the parents weren't ones to be apprehensive about. The way she handled the minefield that was meeting Keith was usually the best indicator of whether or not there would be a second date.

"You don't ever have to worry about that goofy bastard sneaking up on you, do ya Bass?" said Baldy, watching Keith walk away.

No, you didn't. If you were lucky, you would be standing at the rail near the guinea stand when you heard him coming. The horses pass, going the wrong way, some at a walk, some at a trot, some threatening to buck, some kicking up their heals, and all of them Thoroughbreds. I knew I was lucky to be at the track even then.

The horses would backtrack to different spots, some would go to get schooled in the starting gate, the rest would turn, stop, and then begin their exercise regimen. The fast gallopers angled to the inside, the slow gallopers to the outside. I could hear the sound of leather squeaking against leather, the sound of aluminum horseshoes striking the pavement behind me, muted hoofbeats in front of me, the smell of fresh dirt and cigarette smoke wafting through the air on a perfect morning in June...Damn. There is no place I would rather be. It is a thrill to win a race, but the outside rail on the backstretch in the morning is where I would be content to spend eternity.

By this time, I would be listening less and watching more as my horse galloped by, his neck bowed, snorting as he exhaled with every stride, his clearly defined muscles rippling, his sleek brown coat shining in the morning sun. It gives me chills a little bit, just remembering that horse, that time, and those people.

"Is that a tractor I hear?" asked Lou Spence, in a slow Kentucky sounding accent.

"No, Lou," said Baldy. "It's your head rattling."

I didn't see any tractors. Or hear them. What I saw was a good looking little brown Thoroughbred on the track.

I would watch as Officer's Citation went into the far turn, around and into the stretch. He looked like he was all legs, casting a long shadow as he galloped down the stretch while the sun climbed the sky behind us. I would lose sight of him as he went in front of the tote board, and across the finish line. I would hear again the horsemen and women, laughing, talking, and cursing. Officer's Citation would gallop past us slowly one last time, and I would almost be in a catatonic state, I was getting so mesmerized by this horse.

As Marv said, "they all look a little bit better when they're in your barn."

Officer's Citation did look good. He was hardly breaking a sweat during his workouts by this time, just two weeks away from a race. Leonard would pull him up at the end of the stretch, and I would watch him make his way to the gap. He would turn and face the track, looking like a bronze statue with his ears pricked forward, not moving a muscle until Leonard finished rubbing his neck and mane and gave him the signal to head for the barn.

So it went for the rest of the week, Officer's Citation getting more fit with every stride, his muscles becoming more pronounced, his skin tight and sleek against his skin. Not a pimple on him, as the saying went around the racetrack. I always liked the fact that he had no white markings, just a little brown horse with a black mane, tail, and legs, and the disposition of a happy puppy dog.

Friday finally arrived. Work days were always a little more fun.

I removed the rings from the reins in preparation for our first four-furlong work, stretching out from three furlongs to a half mile. Leonard didn't change much of his routine, maybe going a little slower as he galloped around the track the first time. Officer's Citation was in what was called a straight dee snaffle bit, which did little to stop a horse who didn't want to be controlled but was perfect for a young veteran like Officers Citation. It was the least intrusive bit you could use on a horse on the track.

The half-mile pole at Playfair was about two-thirds of the way around the clubhouse turn, and Leonard let him pick up some speed as he passed the nine-sixteenths pole, rolling into the work nice and easy. Leonard was pretty high in the irons, straining against a horse that wanted to run. He had thrown a pretty short cross, but Officer's Citation was on the muscle and striding out well as he galloped past the guinea stand.

Baldy said quietly, "get ahold of him, Leonard," as Officer's Citation ran by.

It was a pretty steady work, Leonard winning the battle of wills with Officer's Citation by a nose. The horse galloped out free and easy, pulled up near the quarter pole and then trotted back to the gap, not quite as willing to stand still when he turned back to the track just as a working horse sped by. Officer's Citation grabbed the bit and took a couple jumps toward the rail, wanting to race the horse who was now working.

Leonard got control of him, brought him back to the gap and repeated the ritual, finally getting the horse to stand still before turning and exiting the track. "The son of a bitch has run on his mind," Baldy said to me. "Get the time, would you Bass?"

I called up to the clockers tower, asking what they caught Officer's Citation in. Forty-nine flat came back the answer. As I walked next to the horse back to the barn, Leonard asked what the time was, and winced when he heard forty-nine. Too fast, and he knew he could catch hell from Baldy. He was correct, but Baldy was having a hard time disguising how happy he was with this horse.

"Got the bulge on you from the jump, didn't he?" Baldy asked Leonard. "What'd he go in, Bass, forty-five and change?"

"Forty-nine flat."

"He must have walked past the finish line then, as fast as he went by us."

Leonard was taking his abuse in good stride, understanding the point years before he got the current lecture.

Leonard knew Baldy was pleased and he said, "Did it pretty easy, though."

"Yeah," said Baldy. "Probably because no one was pulling back on the reins."

Leonard didn't respond. He just said "We okay, Bass?" as he looked the horse over.

"Looks like it. He didn't turn a hair." I said, the terminology meaning he hardly broke a sweat. Trying to sound like I knew something.

Leonard had unsaddled the horse, and I removed his bridle and got him into his halter and took him to the wash rack, giving him a couple of swallows of water in the stall before we went.

I washed him slowly and gently, running the sponge over his skin, applying a light touch so as not to irritate his skin or aggravate any body soreness he might have, taking the time to inspect every inch of his body. I didn't know if he was fast or not, but he was a damn good looking horse. I headed across the pavement to begin stripping the stall, stopping every five minutes or so to give my horse a drink of water. just four or five swallows at a time, no matter how much he wanted to drink.

I finished the stall, raked the shedrow, tossed him a can of oats, and sat down with Baldy to admire the horse for a few minutes until it was time to put him in. I finished watering and cooling him out, and then walked with Baldy slowly back to the cafe, where we ran into my boss, Bill Rizzuto.

"The kid's going to be late today, Bill," Baldy said, "We got some shit to discuss over breakfast."

Bill looked at me and back to Baldy, and said to me, "Mitcheltree needs a couple of sacks of oats as soon as we can get them there."

"Sounds like you better get a wheelbarrow and get down there then," Baldy said to Bill.

This did not help my relationship with Bill as far as employers and employees go, but it was pretty fun.

"I can carry a sack to him real quick and tell him the rest will be here by eleven, will that work?" I asked Bill, the reality being I needed and wanted the job.

"Nah, I'll get it," Bill said. "Go have breakfast."

One and One

Colin, undefeated champion and Horse of the Year in 1908

Times really don't matter in racing, as the surface changes every day. Any change in the moisture content of the dirt will affect the surface, which will affect the times. Some tracks are consistent, some are not. Playfair had a good track man, a buddy of Marv's named Earl. I believe they met working construction while building roads or bridges, not at the track.

Earl was a good dirt man, and the surface was good. The only problem was the banking on the turns, and even the stretch was a little too high. This was done at the direction of management, and for the purpose of getting the water to run off the track when it rained. The slope tended to make the horse's back sore over time.

Another variant was the pace of the race. It is said at the track, 'pace makes the race,' and it is true. If the pacesetter can get to the front and then very subtly slow down without being passed, he dramatically improves his chances of getting to the wire first. If he can win, the time is usually slow in the cheaper claiming ranks, and faster as the horses get better. Bad riders try to get a quarter in twenty-two seconds, good riders try to steal a quarter in twenty-four seconds.

But if a horse sprints to the front immediately and just keeps going, chances are he will eventually run out of gas, the pace will collapse, and the closers will come running at the end. Better horses can run further faster, and generally, any race at a mile or less is won by the front runner at the highest levels of the sport. As the claiming prices get cheaper, the distance a horse can sprint gets shorter.

According to Tesio, stamina is nothing more than sustaining speed over a longer distance. It makes me wonder if breeding for speed exclusively has its origins in that simple statement, considering how Tesio-created bloodlines dominate the sport today. (The Kentucky Derby favorite in 2019 will probably be Omaha Beach, and he is a direct descendant of Tesio's stallion, Nearco, through one of Northern Dancer's most prolific sons, Danzig. This is a powerhouse bloodline Tesio and his unconventional methods created.)

Sprinters tend to suffer more injuries than horses who run at a mile or further. Sprinting is a brutal way for a horse to make a living. Sometimes sprinters hurt themselves just because of how fast they run. Sometimes they get injured simply due to the physics of running through a narrow opening between two horses moving at nearly forty miles an hour.

Marv and Baldy preferred route horses and loved the marathon races. But there weren't many marathons, and generally, it took a tougher horse than we had to win. There were plenty of races for a cheap condition horse who needed to route, however.

You had to sprint before you could stretch them out, and the trick was to keep your horse relaxed while he was sprinting because it is very important to have a relaxed horse in a route race. In fact, a relaxed horse usually made everything easier on everyone, including the horse.

The morning after the half-mile work, I got to the barn at the usual time, around seven. No problem with the stall chains, as I had expected the work to take something out of him. I undid the bottom chain and ducked under it into his stall. He had cleaned up his feed, which was a very good sign.

I wouldn't be able to check for heat this particular morning due to the mud on his legs. I applied the mud, and using aluminum foil or saran wrap, wrapped the leg so the heat stayed in and the mud stayed wet. A squeak from the saran wrap can get a groom kicked quicker that he can say uh-oh. Aluminum foil is a high-risk proposition with every twitch and crinkle, so I used saran wrap. Over the saran wrap, I would wrap the entire leg with two ace bandages, and secure them with clips, safety pins, or electrical tape. I used a light but firm touch while wrapping legs; a bandage wound too tightly can cause a bow. Once the bandages are applied, all that is left to do is hope you don't come back to a tangled up mess in the morning.

I would lie awake at night visualizing an upside down horse hog-tied like a calf at the rodeo. When these visions persisted, I would find myself driving to the track at two in the morning just to make sure. Two in the morning was also a nice, quiet time to be at the racetrack. I always liked it best when it was quiet and no one was around.

But I arrived at seven that morning, and seeing no damage, I unwrapped the bandages and threw them outside by the stall door. I carefully unwrapped the saran wrap and attached the shank to his halter with the snap, just like a lead rope on the saddle horses at home.

Marv always said, "You take these Thoroughbreds by the head at all times."

I had a tired horse though, and I was just taking him to the walker. I had ahold of the shank about halfway down, just casually holding on.

I started out the stall when Officer's Citation lunged forward and hit me square in the back with his chest, lifting me off my feet and thankfully throwing me to the left out of his way. I was okay, but was still in a rodeo, hanging on to the end of a shank with a wild horse on the end of it. He hit the end of the shank and it spun him around facing me, and he then reared straight up and pawed at the air. It would have been beautiful if I were able to enjoy it more. And as suddenly as it started, it stopped.

He came down, kicked once with both hind feet, then settled down and looked at me like 'what are you worried about?'

I took him back into the stall and put the shank over his nose, and then snapped another lead rope to his halter so I could tie him at the wash rack. That accomplished, I headed out the stall about a hundred and thirty percent more alert than I was a minute ago. The echo of Marv's words admonishing me to 'take these thoroughbreds by the head' kept ringing in my ears.

I could still describe Officer's Citation as a horse with a good disposition, but I certainly couldn't describe him as gentle anymore. He was ready to run as far as he was concerned. I was ready to listen to everything Marv and Baldy said. I got a lesson that day, and I was lucky it wasn't a disaster. "Play your tension," was always Marv's advice.

I tied the horse at the wash rack and ran cold water on his legs until the mud was nearly gone. I rubbed the stubborn areas gently with my hand to get the legs totally clean, finally putting him on the walker about twenty minutes later. He didn't raise much hell, but every once in a while he would lunge forward and kick at the moon with both hind feet. He was feeling good, but he was getting the weekend off no matter what.

Regardless of what came Sunday, he was going to be a tiger Monday morning. I wanted to walk him longer to settle him down a little, but it was having the opposite of the intended effect. I put him back in the stall, did his feet up with Hooflex and lanolin, and went to the rail where I spent the rest of the morning.

He was tougher Sunday than he was Saturday, but since I was usually alone on his days off, I got there at about six in the morning. I hung him on the walker and cleaned his stall, and had to change out every brass snap on the chains. The zinc was holding. He was still kicking the walls and charging the chains on a regular basis, but the snap system was working.

The longer he was on the walker, the more revved up he got. His legs were cold, he cleaned up a full ration of feed from the night before, and dove into his breakfast like he hadn't eaten for a week. He was starting to act like a bully, relaxed and on the muscle.

If a saddle horse acted this way, you would take measures to get control, but it wasn't quite so simple with a racehorse. They had to still know that you were in charge, but it was better if they were raising hell as opposed to being docile and obedient.

Officer's Citation was demanding to go back to the track, and he would have to raise hell for another twenty-four hours before he got his wish. I could see that the guy at the tack shop was going to make his week just selling snaps to me.

I spent the rest of the morning at the rail, watching the horses work, taking it all in, still not quite aware that I was the luckiest man on the planet, but starting to get an inkling. I would like to say I was getting to know the horses by watching the works, but I couldn't identify any of them just by looking, and while I knew a lot of the trainers, I still couldn't put very many names to the faces. 'Hey buddy' usually sufficed as a conversation starter.

Every once in a while, a majestic, muscular specimen would walk by and I would wonder, "who the hell is that?" Nine times out of ten, it was a horse who had been or still was a stakes horse. There was a big gray horse training at the track, and I knew who he was on sight. His name was Captain Condo, and he was the best on the grounds, about ten lengths faster than the next best horse. He was in the early stages of a career that would last for nearly ten years and make him a legend in the Pacific Northwest.

Captain Condo ended up earning in excess of a quarter million dollars, most of it in Seattle or Spokane, a very respectable total anywhere, and twice as impressive in the northwest, where the money ain't, in terms of horse racing.

He had a full sister who was just as big and beautiful and she didn't accomplish much of anything on the track. You just never knew.

It was almost better hanging out at the rail without a horse on the track. I would take in all the sights and the sounds, the muted hoofbeats of the horses pounding the track. The sound of the starting gate opening and the bell ringing as the young horses were being schooled; the beauty of the infield at Playfair. The barn swallows flying, sometimes pacing the horses as they galloped. The perfect temperatures of a late June morning in the inland empire. The horses would trot by, the riders bouncing on the saddle or standing in the irons, hustling to get done because they had two more to get out before the break.

At Playfair Race Course, the path across the infield was dirt, covered with tree bark, and lined with ten or twelve-foot tall juniper bushes. When I led my horse across after the race, it smelled like I was walking through a forest full of Christmas trees. The entire infield was covered with green grass and was well watered and well maintained. In the spring when the flowers were in bloom, it was highlighted with patches of red bulbs, as well as other different colored flowers and bulbs. The way these colors accented the red and green made the entire infield burst with color. Spokane is the Lilac City, so there was plenty of purple, and nothing smells quite as good as a lilac bush in full bloom.

I have never seen a small track that had an infield that

beautiful, and not very many large tracks, at least not the newer ones. At that time, the grandstand was an ugly yellow color, but the entire scene was as pretty as a postcard picture as you looked across the infield from the backstretch to the grandstand.

I had Sundays off, from the job but not the horse, and post time for the first race on Sunday was one o'clock, so the track usually closed for training at nine. I went for breakfast at the cafe and was studying my racing form. Intending to kill three hours finding some good bets and getting to the front side in time to watch yesterdays replays, a light bulb suddenly went off in my head. I slammed the rest of my half-order breakfast and headed back to the barn.

I could see the system was working when I got back to the barn. He was stretching the brass snaps, but the energy dispersed by the stretching brass enabled the zinc to hold. Zinc was not stronger than brass, just less flexible. Had I used all zinc, I imagined they would have shattered and the pieces wouldn't have hit the ground before a grand looking little brown horse was running around loose in the barn area.

I retrieved a shank out of the tack shed and went to the stall. I put the chain over his noseband on the halter he was wearing, and fastened the snap underneath the halter. This method gave me a little more control than just the leadrope, and could be converted to a lipchain if things went completely to hell.

I leaned against him as he pushed me out of the stall, if for no other reason than to lessen the impact of the potential lunge. We turned left and walked north to where there was a sand pit, and I gave him some slack as he put his nose to the ground and buckled his knees so that he could roll in the sand.

He rolled and squirmed on the ground for a few minutes before practically leaping up and shaking himself, engulfing both of us in a cloud of dust, showing me what he thought of being clean and indicating to me that he had no back problems, as a sore horse usually won't roll.

We headed further north to a patch of green grass, Officer's Citation with his ears pricked forward, looking side to side, taking in his unfamiliar surroundings, walking so easily I could barely feel him on the end of the shank. He knew what grass was, though, and led me for the last ten yards.

I let him graze for about an hour, quickly and nervously at first, but then he gradually settled down as he realized we had no deadline. I then showed him the rest of the barn area, where all I made grain deliveries, the restrooms in case he ever tried the biscuits and gravy.

I even took a few orders from feed customers who needed grain before the backstretch was closed for deliveries during the races. I didn't mind, we had a warehouse about six furlongs from the track, and I went and put my horse back in his stall, refilled his hay net and water bucket, and got the customers their grain before the races.

Who knows if I did any good gambling at the track that day. I wasn't a very good gambler. It was a good day regardless of the money I probably lost. One year I made it a policy to not buy a beer until I cashed a winning ticket, and I damned near stopped drinking altogether.

After the races, I fed Officer's Citation, walked him for about fifteen minutes while I picked the turds out of his stall, and put a happy and relaxed horse to bed for the night.

I looked at the mound of vitamins on top of the mountain of grain he was about to eat and reminded myself to be ready for a bullying contest tomorrow morning. I was as anxious as he was to go back to the track. I said goodnight, and headed for home.

Monday brought everything I expected, and I had a handful of horse to deal with in the stall, just as Leonard had a handful on the track. I asked Leonard if we should shorten the rings a notch, and he was polite enough to ignore the insult. He just smiled and said he thought we would be alright. He was right, but he said I might have had the right idea when they came off the track. Officer's Citation was getting to be pretty tough as he approached peak physical condition.

Officer's Citation had settled down after his grazing and tour of the barnyard, and I tried to get him out whenever I had some spare time after that. He was still tough to handle, but he gradually settled down throughout the week, and finally, the Friday that would end up changing my life had arrived.

That morning, I arrived at five thirty, anxious to get going. I was doubly diligent about checking his legs for heat, his body for soreness or inflammation, the hair on his mane for signs of dandruff.

I was like a bicycle mechanic inspecting a Ferrari, having no idea what I was looking for, but discovering that it all looked good. I pulled his water bucket and gave him just a handful of grain for breakfast. He'd gotten used to eating well and always wanted more. He could have all he wanted later.

I took the rings off the reins and rinsed the bit, cleaned the headgear as best I could, raked the shedrow and got the hell away from my horse for a while.

I went up to the cafe and had a leisurely breakfast for a change. I was getting tired of the Backstretch Scramble, but I was way too superstitious to change my order.

Finally, after what seemed like ages, Baldy arrived. It may have been forty-five minutes, but I don't remember being so anxious for a work before or since. I got our coffees and we walked toward the barn.

"Been to the stall?" Baldy asked.

"I got here about five-thirty," I said.

"Jesus," Baldy said. "Go to the tack shop and get another shank and some blinkers."

Blinkers are a hood with holes cut for the eyes and cups attached behind the eye-holes, restricting a horse's vision and keeping them focused by not letting the horse see anything that might distract them.

I had taken two steps toward the tack shop before I realized he was talking about using them on me.

I took his point and tried to settle down. I'm not sure blinkers were the solution anyway, I was pretty focused.

I didn't ask about the shank.

Baldy staggered up to the stall, and stagger, stagger, clip, clop, smack, the tradition repeated itself. "Any problems?" he asked.

"Ice cold," I replied.

Baldy gritted his teeth and nodded. Habitually. Often. Almost like he was shaking, but he was just quickly and barely nodding his head for a few seconds at a time, sometimes a half a minute.

"Get the cheap son of a bitch tacked in case the gallop boy shows up," he said.

As I brushed him, I assured Officer's Citation he wasn't cheap, he was four by four to War Admiral and a direct descendant of the perfect Thoroughbred Ribot, Undefeated European champion. And let's not forget the maternal grandsire, Citation, who more than a few loud voices might argue was the greatest of all time. It was all part of putting a poultice on his heart.

I didn't mention to him that his last purchase price was eight hundred dollars. That was pretty cheap for any horse, much less a racehorse, even then.

That damned unreliable gallop boy showed up ten minutes before the renovation break ended, just like he did every single day, like clockwork. If you are going to be unreliable, his is the way to do it. Baldy and Leonard didn't have a lot to discuss as far as the work was concerned. They had worked together for more than a few years, and other than distance, the only other directive would be to go slow. "Easy, God damnit," is how Baldy would have said it.

I led the horse out. He stayed cool and knew he was finally going to the track. He tossed his head a little, not feeling the restriction of the rings. He reminded me of an athlete beginning to stretch his muscles in preparation for the work.

I turned Officer's Citation loose, Leonard in control, and his pace quickened, but he walked through the gap and past us on the rail calm and cool.

I called up to the clocker, pointed to my horse and said, "Officer's Citation, five-eighths."

I was trying to figure out why I was so anxious for this work but wrote it off to being the last one before entering him in a race. I must have seen something in the half-mile work that I wasn't even aware of, in retrospect.

Marv and Baldy, both good poker players, never tipped their hands to me. They never indicated to me what they thought, good or bad, about the way things were going.

I watched as Officer's Citation trotted about halfway to the starting gate, and then they turned and stopped. I have a picture in my mind of him standing perfectly still for a full minute, his ears pricked forward, surveying the scene. I saw him take a deep breath, lower and shake his head as he trotted for two steps and went straight into his slow gallop.

Officer's Citation went past us, neck bowed and pulling against Leonard, but not fighting him, the textbook definition of relaxed and on the muscle. He went by slowly the first time, into and out of the far turn, still going slow, still on the outside, and Leonard had him facing slightly away from the inside rail. The only indication of what was to come was that the horse would pop his tail in the air, shake his head, and pull at the reins when a horse would work past him on the inside.

They were at the eighth pole, almost out of sight behind the tote board when Leonard straightened Officer's Citation out and started angling to the inside rail. The last I saw as he disappeared was Leonard checking for traffic on the inside as he let out another notch on the reins.

A five-furlong work was once around the bullring. Officer's Citation re-appeared just after crossing the finish line, well into stride, his neck bowed, still obeying Leonard but wanting to run. Baldy had told me when we started watching the horses together, watch the poles that supported the rail to get an indication of speed. I watched them as my horse went by. He looked like he was exerting no more effort than when he slow galloped. While I had seen the poles click by that fast before, he sure looked like he was going easy.

Leonard gave him a little more rein as they neared the quarter pole, and in the space of the next twenty-two seconds, my entire way of thinking changed forever. My brain was about to be re-wired.

I didn't know why, but as he approached the three-sixteenths, I started getting chills racing up from the bottom of my spine to the top of my head, and It felt like my face was on fire. In fact, my entire body was on fire, and it was like every one of my senses except for sight shut down and applied themselves to only what I was seeing, and I didn't really know what that was. But something was happening. I felt it as much as I saw it. The poles were flying by, and Officer's Citation's stride was just fluid and easy. I remember looking over as the horse passed the eighth pole, and saw Baldy holding on to the rail, staggering a little bit, his face flushed and grinning from ear to ear.

Baldy's reaction confirmed what I felt but did not understand. I imagined that this was what the first rip of heroin felt like to the addict. I loved this and I wanted a lot more of it.

The last I saw before the tote board obscured Officer's Citation would be best described as him shifting gears because it looked like his stride lengthened twenty inches as he passed the sixteenth pole.

I couldn't see the horse, but the rider was visible, and a friend of Baldy's in the guinea stand had a stopwatch on him. He told us Officer's Citation went the last eighth in eleven seconds flat. Under a pretty good hold, too.

Leonard was standing in the irons and pulling back, and the horse galloped out with his ears pricked, looking finer than anything I have ever seen in my life.

I still wasn't sure I would ever know what it was to win a race, but I knew suddenly and immediately what addiction was all about. I was hooked. I looked over and saw Baldy trying hard to get the grin off his face before Leonard and Officer's Citation returned to the gap.

The horse wasn't even breathing hard as he came off the track, and I was so stunned, I didn't even think to ask for the time.

Baldy called up to the tower and said, "What did you catch Officer's Citation in?"

"One and one," came the reply, "bullet so far."

Baldy gritted his teeth when he heard bullet. He wasn't mad

at anyone but the clocker, for it was an easy work, and easy bullet works are not conducive to long odds, which is where the Putzier Brothers liked to run their horses. Tough, ready, and meriting little respect from the gamblers was how they preferred it all play out. They loved cashing big tickets and probably suspected they had a chance to do so with this horse. I personally had no idea. I was in a daze, with tunnel vision and laser beam focus on my horse. Baldy headed for the stall and I met Leonard and Officer's Citation coming off the track.

"How much?" Leonard asked.

"One and one," I replied. The time was one minute, one second, and one fifth.

Leonard grimaced, which was becoming traditional when the horse worked. "He had a gear or two left," he said to me.

"Baldy looked pretty happy, but don't tell him I said so," I said to Leonard as I put my hand on the shoulder of my horse. He had broken only a little sweat and wasn't breathing hard at all. I didn't know anything, but I was pretty sure he was fit enough to race.

I stepped back just so I could watch him walk, and I got the same chill one more time. It was like in a movie when you see a starship transitioning to light speed, stars whizzing past, creating a vignette of my horse walking back to the barn. I thought I was going to pass out.

"Bass," Baldy said, snapping me partially out of my trance. "Get some water for that poor son of a bitch, Leonard just tried to break a track record."

Leonard grinned. So did I, and in spite of himself, so did Baldy.

"Keep your mouth shut, Bass, and we might cash a gamble," Baldy said.

Taking A Hold

*Playfair program from 1964 Harvest Handicap. The Putzier Bros.
won the race with #3, Stiltz*

I don't exactly remember how tough Officer's Citation was that Saturday morning, but his groom had an extra bounce to his step, I can assure you of that. Officer's Citation's legs, ankles, and knees were still cold, and, true to his habit, he had cleaned up his feed.

There were no setbacks, and the next step was to find him a race. It would be his first race, but it would also serve as his final work.

Available to all owners, trainers, and potential owners, was a small book you could pick up at the race office called a condition book. The Racing Secretary, licensed by the state racing commission, writes the condition book, which would eventually provide every racehorse on the grounds with a race they were eligible to enter.

Claiming races make up the bulk of the program, and they are the lower level races, but graduate in price up to the allowance class races, which are one level below the stakes races. A handicap race is a race where the weight the horses carry is assigned to horses likely to run in a stakes race.

There is very little point in explaining stakes and allowance races in this journal, for my little horse would have had to sprout wings to be eligible for either. His average earnings per start the previous year were one hundred fifty-five dollars per start.

The lowest claiming price, or agreed selling price of any horse entered in a claiming race at Playfair, was twenty-five hundred dollars. That meant that if you enter your horse in a $2500 claiming race, any licensed owner or trainer can purchase the horse for the claiming price. The trainer does this by filling out what is called a claim slip and depositing it in the claim box in the paddock fifteen minutes prior to the scheduled post time.

The starting gate is the post, so post time is the scheduled start time of the race. The claiming trainer is liable for the horse as soon as the horse is declared a starter, which is as soon as the starting gate opens without malfunctioning.

The entering trainer is responsible for the horse he sold until the results from the testing facility are declared legal. If the horse is injured during the race, the claiming trainer is on the hook, and if he is tested and found to have illegal drugs in his system, with the selling trainer is where the consequences will fall.

As long as the money has been deposited in the race office, the claim is declared valid but may be disputed by the purchasing trainer.

What this system does is provide a way for horses to run against horses with equal talent. A horse's optimum claiming level is referred to as his class, and the lowest level is called the bottom.

Further conditions are assigned, such as maiden races, for horses who have never won a race in their life. Never won two, and never won three are self-explanatory graduated conditions. If a horse runs through his conditions, or wins three races, he is only eligible for what are referred to as open races, usually only restricted by age and sex. Maiden, never won two, and never won three are referred to as condition races, and if a horse is eligible for condition races, he is said to still have conditions.

Condition races are easier because some of the horses who end up in open races at the bottom can be tough old horses who aren't quite as good as they once were but can still race and win. This type of horse was fun to have, but I wouldn't know that for a few more years.

Unfortunately, there is no point in explaining anything that happened above the bottom claiming level in 1987, because near the bottom is where we started, and near the bottom is where we stayed. There were some highs and lows along the way, however. I learned a little bit about what the difference was between being disappointed in running seventh, as opposed to second. Usually about a hundred bucks, is the answer.

There is a saying in the racing world, keep yourself in the best company, and your horses in the worst.

To address the second part first, find the class where your horse can win. Marv called it putting a price on your horse. Since eight hundred is less than twenty-five hundred, the bottom was the bottom, and we would have to improve our horse to get there. And since never won two is what we had, we were looking for bottom level never won two condition races to enter. The bottom was $2500 claiming in the open races, but in the condition races, sometimes the bottom was $3200 or $4000.

As far as keeping yourself in the best company, you can go a long way toward accomplishing this by simply avoiding jock agents. I was going to add a qualifier to that but the only one that comes to mind is unless he owes you money.

We were in Barbara's Backstretch Cafe, and a trainer by the name of Joe Borg came by and sat down with us. I was introduced, the signal for this guy is ok and worth knowing. He was one of us, he was a good fella. Maybe not quite that, but respect meant an introduction. Baldy, in the course of breakfast, asked Joe how he did in Portland last winter.

"That God damned place. I am so sick of the mud and bullshit," Joe said. "I think we win two all winter."

Baldy nodded his head, they discussed other things, and Joe left.

Baldy said to me after Joe was gone, "You got a shitter can run mud, you splash along pretty happy in that wet son of a bitch."

"I bet a horse with Ribot in his pedigree would do ok down there," I said, having by this time become an unorthodox student of both 'The Daily Racing Form', and whatever stallion registry and pedigree books I could get my hands on. Also, I was trying to indicate that I might be paying attention.

"It don't hurt," he said. "But our good mud runners weren't all bred to run mud. They were strong because we slow gallop. It's isometrics, they pull against themselves and build muscle. Strong horses run deep tracks better than weak horses, that's just a fact. Plus every asshole out there is convinced that you have to send your horse as hard as they can go in the mud. If we had a pace in every race like we had in the Washington Championship, Stiltz would have been undefeated."

Jockeys, with their tack, or saddle and equipment the horse will carry on his back, are weighed immediately before and after every race they compete in. Carl Schilling, the jockey who rode Stiltz for the Putzier Brothers in the Washington Championship in 1964, gained seven pounds during the race, all of it mud.

The write up in the Washington Horse magazine said, "Stiltz, the only horse with no chance of winning the Washington Championship, did." Stiltz went from last to first and won pretty easily. A friend of Baldy's had a stack of hundred dollar win tickets on Stiltz.

"No chance my ass," said Baldy. "He ran third the next year and got flat out shut off at the quarter pole. Stiltz could handle the Washington-breds."

To his dying day, Marv referred to Schilling's agent as a crook, and that was only if he was being polite. Baldy agreed.

But we still had a race to find.

89

The next condition would be distance, so we were looking for sprints. Racing, as well as training, you have to stretch them out gradually. Preference wise, the Putzier brothers always preferred routing, as opposed to sprinting. It was easier on the horse.

Longer races gave more time for tactical situations to develop. There still existed the potential for the same dangerous situations in routes as sprints, namely the starting gate, and from the quarter pole home. Other than that, there was more time for the horses to spread out and not run in crowds, where the danger lurks. The best opportunities to win races and keep the horse sound were the routes.

We found a race scheduled for Sunday, July 5th, two weeks away. All we had to do was slow gallop another week, one more easy work, and enter on Monday. The conditions were written something like: Horses four years old and older who have never won two races. Distance: 6 furlongs, Claiming Price $2500, Weight 122 Lbs., Fillies and Mares allowed 3 Lbs. Apprentice allowance *5 Lbs, **10 lbs. Purse $1600. Purse distribution: First, 55%, second 20%, third 15%, fourth 7%, and fifth was 3%. Running fifth was referred to as saving the mount, enough to cover the cost of the jock mount, either ten percent of the purse share or $35, whichever was greater. There was no entry fee in claiming races, but the jock mount was a de facto entry fee.

Cheap as they write races, running against the cheapest horses on the grounds, more than likely at long odds. If the Marv and Baldy could write their dream condition, it would be this race going a mile and a sixteenth. And if they thought they could get away with it, they would enter a monster, steal the purse, and tap the till, Marv-speak for cashing on a long shot.

I didn't know this for sure, but judging by all the pictures of winners hanging on the wall from the first foray into the racing business, I just sort of assumed that this was the path we were on. Win pictures have both a picture of the horse running at the wire, and standing in the winner's circle. I never gave much thought to photographers in 1987.

But sometimes the photograph would capture the Totalizator, or 'tote' board. The tote board showed the number of the horse in the program, current odds updated at the bell, or when the race starts and no more bets are accepted. It also showed the amounts of money wagered on every betting option, and the totals in the various pools; hence "tote" board.

I tended to look at the horse at the wire, study the horse in the winner's circle, and see what the odds and payoff were. Some of them were big and usually came with a good story. Whenever I show someone a winner's circle picture, they ask about the people if they ask anything at all. I suppose it is because they can already see the horse's name.

Marv and Baldy were pretty sure they had the horse and the odds for the gamble, and knew they could get it done at this distance. The only unknown was whether or not the horse would fire his shot, or not make any mistakes and run to his ability first start of the year.

Working your horse out of the starting gate can mitigate this variable. Marv and Baldy never did this if they had a gate approved horse, not wanting to take chances on ending up with a horse who didn't like going to the starting gate, or getting 'gate sour'. It also puts unnecessary stress on the legs and back to break from a standing start. It also opened the door to getting put on the Starter's list for bad behavior, which requires a work from the starting gate for re-approval. It was better for a good gate horse to use his first race as his gate work.

The chance you were taking was that your horse would bounce out of the gate alertly and win the race at long odds, and the only ticket you are holding could only be exchanged for one beer. It was a problem you might lament while sipping reflectively on that beer, but you wouldn't necessarily complain about it. Winning is winning, and provided the taps are clean, it could be worse. Without a gate work, the racehorse is usually off a little slow in his first race of the season, but not always. I tended to bet no matter what I thought might happen, just in case something good did happen. This meant that I was always covered and frequently broke.

At around seven in the morning, I would walk through the cafe, get a coffee and the latest racing form, walk to the barn, toss Officer's Citation a can of oats, and repair damaged snaps.

I would then check his legs for heat, do a once-over for anything that might be wrong, and either head to the rail to loiter and listen, or go up to the cafe to eat, loiter, and listen while I waited for Baldy to arrive.

When Baldy would arrive, I would get two coffees to go, and we would walk back to the barn. Once there, I would pick Officer's Citation's feet, brush his mane and tail, and tack him up in time to go to the track right after the renovation break.

As soon as the announcement came over the PA, I would leg Leonard up in the stall, follow them to the gap, and spend the best twenty minutes of the day watching a powerful athlete train and strain against his rider.

Then, Officer's Citation would finish his exercise, come off the track out of the gap, and Leonard and I would exchange 'everything ok's'.

Leonard would then go about his business, I would hang Officer's Citation on the walker, and clean his stall. I would cool him out, put him away, give him a quick rubdown, and head back to the rail. Or I would just hang around the barn before it was time to go to work.

It was the routine, and it was the best way in the world to spend any morning.

There were not any notable events that I recall during that week.

The fina work was a half mile in forty-nine and change, nice and easy, and everything went like clockwork.

"Your shitter is taking a hold," Baldy said, gritting his teeth and nodding his head.

Chum Salmon

Marikaye, in the center

One New Year's Eve in the late eighties or early nineties, I was
going to escort a beautiful young lady I went to high school with
to a party somewhere in Seattle. I don't have any recollection

of where we went or what we did, and so I can only conclude that it was a very good party.

What I do remember, possibly because it was early in the evening, was driving over to the house she lived in, where she was renting a room from her employer, and I'm pretty sure his name was Joe.

I arrived and went to the door. Joe let me in and invited me to sit down as he settled into his recliner. On my way to the couch, I noticed a trophy with a racehorse on top of it.

Stopping, I asked, "What is that?"

"Oh, come on, no," said my date, Marikaye, as she entered the room and heard us talking horses.

Joe said the trophy was won by a horse he and some partners had owned a few years before.

"What was the name of the horse?" I asked.

Marikaye was pretty tired of racehorses by now. She and I hung out a lot, and every analogy she heard come out of my mouth since June of 1987, and there were a lot of them, had something to do with racehorses.

"He was a pretty good horse," said Joe. "We bought him through the sale when he was a two year old, and he ended up winning the Portland Mile, and the Longacres Mile in 1985."

"No kidding," I said, fully committed to discussing racehorses with Joe for the next few hours. "Who was it?"

"We gotta go," said Marikaye, who had seen all this before.

"Chum Salmon," said Joe.

"He's Chum Salmon," I said, Imitating the announcers call from the race a few years before. I'd seen a replay of the Longacres mile Chum Salmon won but I didn't see the race live.

"We gotta go," said Marikaye.

"I got the tape of the Longacres Mile," my new best friend Joe said.

"Man, I would love to see that."

"We don't have time."

"Hunny Bunny, " I said, "It takes a minute and thirty-four seconds."

Joe suddenly knew I was serious.

"Thirty-three and change," he said, springing up and out of the recliner. "I'll get the tape."

I got the look, and Joe got the cassette loaded into the VCR.

"We're going to be late," said Marikaye.

"No, we'll close with a late rush and get up just in time," I said, having some fun with the 1981 Spokane International Boat Show Queen, pictured.

Marikaye might not be all that happy with me if she ever reads this book, but I did tell her thirty years ago I was going to write it, so maybe we will be okay.

We, Marikaye and I, met the first day of eighth grade when my parents had just moved our family to Oakesdale. She was the first person I saw when I got on the school bus on the first day of school.

Later that year, still in the infancy of our alliance, she copied my work while we were taking a science test, and I wrote in really big letters to make it easier for her. We both got a D minus and a lecture, but since it was such a bad grade, the teacher figured we both had learned our lesson.

We had, indeed. If you are going to cheat, don't be greedy, was the lesson we took home. We were thrilled with the outcome. I didn't think I'd hit thirty percent on that test, but we ran big and saved the jock mount, barely.

Our bond was strengthened by the science experiment, as we

came to refer to it. Marikaye ended up being the best friend I ever had, and I even worked for her dad on his farm for a couple years. While he was harvesting test loads of wheat, she would read Harlequin romance novels. She had a large paper bag full of them. I read six of them with her one day.

The tape squiggled and showed a test pattern, and then we were watching the start of the post parade for the 1985 Longacres Mile.

This would be Marikaye's place to interject, but she was busy maintaining a frosty silence.

Joe, well tuned by now to the signals of the former District Manager for all the hair salons in Frederick and Nelson department stores in the Spokane/Coeur d 'Alene area, said, "I'll fast forward through this."

Marikaye was a power broker at a young age and knew how to command authority and respect. She could also be a little volatile at times, if you know what I mean. The thing is, she was my buddy long before any of the power brokering ever took place. You either had to be very careful with her or all the way over the top.

I chose over the top. Skating full speed onto the thin ice, I said, "No, I need to see who he ran against."

"Colin Dale," said Marikaye, in a dangerously low tone.

Joe looked back and forth between us, not used to seeing Marikaye challenged, and doubtless ever this successfully. Or else he was thinking I was about to get my head chopped off.

"It's alright," I said to no one in particular, as I was becoming engrossed in the post parade.

Joe tentatively sat down.

So did Marikaye, but I hesitate to call it tentatively. Maybe not forcefully, but in such a way that you could really feel her presence. I mean really feel her presence.

I eased myself on to the couch beside her and moved in unison with her when she tried to move away. I had seen THIS movie before. I stretched and put my arm around her, first date movie theatre style, as I watched the post parade intently. I gradually squeezed her tighter and began to put my other arm around her so I could engulf her in a passive-aggressive bear hug.

"Colin Dale," she said, sternly, through clenched teeth. "Let go of me!"

Joe was nervous, but Marikaye was about to throw in the towel at the quarter pole.

I had her in a firm but gentle bear hug by now, and I said, "Not until you love me again."

The post parade was coming to an end.

"Love me?" I asked.

Silence.

I didn't let her out of the hug.

"I'll fast forward to the start," Joe said.

I said, "No, I want to see the warm-ups."

"COLIN DALE," Marikaye, finding her voice.

"I gotta work with her," said Joe, fast forwarding to the start of the race like the sensible coward he was.

And so my Hunny Bunny and I, wrapped up in a warm, yet frosty embrace, watched Chum Salmon close with a late rush and get up just in time in a thrilling last to first, come from behind victory in the 1985 Longacres Mile.

"He's Chum Salmon," said track announcer Gary Henson as the big horse crossed the finish line.

"He's Chum Salmon," said I.

"He was a good one," said Joe.

"Can we go now?" asked my fashion model impatiently.

Marikaye let the screen door hit me on the way out. I'm pretty sure it was an accident.

Entry

War Admiral

I was never all that interested in staying around the place where I grew up, on a rented seventeen acres of land in the Palouse country in southeastern Washington state, near the town of Oakesdale. If I was from anywhere else, I might describe it as a farm. But considering that it was surrounded by acres and miles of wheat farms, and I went to school with dozens of kids whose parents owned wheat farms of 1600 acres and more, to me it was never a farm.

We had horses. That is primarily why I never thought of it as a farm, and it made me laugh to think about that right now. I felt like we had more when in reality we had less if it is measured in land ownership.

The Palouse country has a specific breed of horse that originated in the region, bred by the Nez Pierce natives, called the Appaloosa horse. It is said that these horses were bred with the dispositions they have so that the braves would be mad enough to fight by the time they reached the battlefield.

It wasn't a ranch, either, but it had one of those big red barns that you see in paintings of big red barns. Not many cows passed through the gates, but a few. Some hogs, chickens, sheep, dogs, cats,...I think that's it. A few corrals surrounded the barn, and they were usually eighteen inches deep with mud in the lower corner of the corral in the springtime.

When Mt St Helens erupted in 1980, the ash that covered the ground three inches deep solidified the mud and built a beautiful corral that only got better the more it rained. Two fenced pastures about eight acres each stood on either side of a gravel lane that crossed the railroad tracks up by the main road, led across the creek bridge, and then up a small hill to the house.

These two pastures became one when the creek flooded every winter. The creek would go from being two feet wide in the summer to four hundred feet wide every winter and spring we lived there. It looked like the Columbia River when the creek was at flood stage. It took the bridge out that first year and the fence on both sides of the driveway. But it was good for an extra week's vacation from school at least once every year.

That first spring at Oakesdale, my brother and I spent countless hours rolling up strands of barbed wire. We would pull the wire out of the weeds and mud as we rolled, detaching it from the metal posts, four strands of wire for each run. It was probably a mile or two of miserable, muddy, barbed wire, the grass holding on as you tried to pull it from the mud. Every day after school for a month we rolled muddy barbed wire.

The creek ran parallel to the main road and perpendicular to the driveway. The gully it had carved was about twelve feet deep where the driveway crossed it on a wooden bridge, which was sturdy enough to support a fully loaded truck hauling wheat or lentils from the fields surrounding the house. The bridge was about twenty inches higher than the road, maybe slightly less, and a short, steep incline elevated to the bridge from the road at either end.

If the railroad tracks didn't take the muffler off the family sedan, the bridge would.

The county police were nice enough to give my brother and I a ride home one night after introducing us to the criminal justice system as it pertains to underage drinking, and came away from the experience needing a new muffler.

We would warn our friends parents about going slow when they came over, but it was pretty quiet in the backseat of the patrol car that night as the patrolman sped toward the bridge. My brother and I grinned at each other and braced ourselves as we made our approach. We were crammed with three more of our buddies in the backseat of the police cruiser, going about twenty-five miles an hour where five was a little too fast.

The bumper of the patrol car dragged a little as the sharp incline to the bridge appeared, probably gaining twenty inches of elevation in four feet. The front springs of the car bottomed out as we hit the ramp, then the back springs, and then the entire car. There was a grinding sound as the gravel scraped the floorboards. We were pushed down into the seats by the g-force, and then BANG, blap, blap, blap, the muffler went, ripped completely off and left lying in the driveway at the end of the bridge.

I swear, in the next second, it felt like we were air born, kind of a light whooshing sound, and you could hear gravel raining down upon the wooden bridge. I could feel my stomach rise to my throat as the sedan re-discovered gravity, and then, BAM, back to the bottom of the suspension, down in the seat, better than hoped for, and not over yet. We surged forward, and the patrolman, getting tossed around pretty good by now, hit the brakes. Mistake. We slid down the ramp on the other end of the bridge and bottomed out for the third and final time. The Whitman County bridge crew builds a hell of a bridge.

"GOD DAMN IT!"

The patrolmen didn't seem all that happy with us and may have had a few words to say about the bridge crew themselves.

"The way you drive, you were lucky to get across the railroad tracks," Deke said, helpfully.

The driver didn't say anything more and had us moving again, easing slowly up the driveway through the gate at the bottom of the hill, driving up and coming to a stop facing the house.

Of the twelve of us who got arrested that night, Deke was the only one who refused to admit anything and he was never charged. The rest of us had to go to alcohol school.

But the best was yet to come. You could get an indication of how much my Dad had been drinking by how far the cowboy hat he always wore was tipped on his head. Sober was not twelve o clock, it was cocked off a little to the left, down over his left eye just a smidge. But a "snort" as he called a drink, usually a screwdriver, or two into it, the hat would begin to migrate a little further left, a little more down over the eye, and continue to migrate relative to how many snorts found their way down the hatch.

As the patrolmen parked and started to get out, I looked up toward the house from the back of the sedan and saw that the hat was damned near touching his left ear. I looked at Dcke, and we smiled at each other and looked back toward the house. We knew we were in trouble, but we were off the hook until the next morning. The patrolmen might not be so lucky.

I didn't hear the conversation and Marv never said, but the patrolmen didn't say a word as they let us out of the car after talking to him. They looked defeated. Maybe they pitied us, maybe they viewed us as future adversaries, who knows. I bet they didn't know. You had to play Marv's conversations back in your head several times before you noticed there was a forest somewhere behind those trees.

And yet, he would get straight to the point by the most direct route. It was just that no one else knew the road existed. He just had a different way of expressing himself.

He was once pulled over in Helena, Montana, for driving the wrong way on a one-way street late at night.

The officer said, "Did you know you were going the wrong way on a one-way street?"

"No, I didn't," said Marv.

The officer, aiming his flashlight at the one-way sign, said, "Didn't you see the arrows?"

"Arrows?" Marv said, looking quickly over his shoulder. "I didn't even see the Indians!"

Surprised, cowboys usually having a sixth sense where

Indians are concerned.

The first thing he ever said to my mom was, "Hey, Ace, I hear your dad has thirty head of horses." The first line in the love story that made my existence possible.

My grandfather's name was John Thompson, but Marv referred to him as Ben, after a famous old west outlaw named Ben Thompson.

Marv loved the poetry of Black Bart, another famous outlaw. Black Bart would rob Wells-Fargo stage coaches, and leave behind poetry taunting the bank detectives and lawmen. If it had to do with the old west, horses, or horse racing, Marv would be interested. Our family movie nights were either westerns or eight-millimeter home movies of the horse races that my mother had filmed. If it had a horse in it, we could watch it. It drove him nuts when an actor would dismount the wrong side of a horse in a movie.

He looked like he was a part of every horse he ever rode. He was smooth and fluid, loose and in control. When he was on his best horse, Hard Hearted, it was like watching one being with one mind, Marv completely in unison with the horse. He was a cowboy, and it wasn't quite a ranch where I grew up.

For two miserable months, we owned the meanest milk cow in America. To me, fresh butter tastes like getting kicked in the teeth by a cow devil named Buttercup. If she had produced chocolate milk, it might have been worth it. But she didn't produce chocolate milk, she dispensed four gallons a day of pure hatred and evil. Man, I hated that cow.

I don't know what to call it, but it was the place where my education in the nutritional needs of animals, and care for animals in general, continued.

The barn was two fairly wide open halves, with two mangers

105

on either side of a pathway down the center of the barn, and about a twelve-foot wide pen running up each side. We built four stalls about eight feet wide, all open in the back, so we could tie the horses we were unspoiling in at night and grain them. This is where I learned to roll the feed to them. It was the same program as at the racetrack with more corn and fewer B vitamins, but not many changes other than that.

Looking back, I had never really thought about how much shit I had shoveled in life, but it would fill more than a few semi-trailers, I bet. It was a great way to grow up, and while I vaguely appreciated the way and place I grew up, I would always find myself wondering what was over the next hill. I hoped eventually to look across the land and not see amber waves of grain. I didn't know I was looking away from Quarter Horse saddle horses and searching for Thoroughbred racehorses. I didn't think horses would be involved at all.

I had never seen one horse on the feeding program for more than forty-five days, but we were several months past that with Officer's Citation, and he was in full bloom. Nearly every ounce of fat on him had been turned to muscle. We had gone slow, and Baldy said that is how you put a bottom in them, a foundation for the campaign ahead. We had a fit horse who was not a tired horse. He was well rested and sound. It was time to enter.

The entries could be called in from the guard shack at the back gate, so Baldy and I walked up there together, probably on Thursday morning to enter Sunday's race. Baldy told them the race number and the name of the horse. They asked for the name of the rider, and he said, "Open."

That was it. We had just entered a six-furlong race for horses who had never won two races and did not name a rider. This sent agents slithering to the barn, hustling the mount for their riders, which is a method that makes getting spun much less likely. The horse did not have a terrible form from the previous year, but he was no world beater. Whoever came by was expecting to earn thirty-five dollars, and not hoping for any more.

We ended up with Randy Colton, a former leading rider, and a perennial contender for the riding title. Having spent years on the grandstand side, I was familiar with him and it seemed like a good omen that one of the leading riders would be on the horse.

We had slow galloped through Friday and gave Officer's Citation Saturday off. I had been studying the form since it came out on Friday. I would stand in front of the stall and lean against the double snap reinforced chains with my back to the horse, and we began a tradition of handicapping his races together when he came up behind me, put his head over my shoulder, and nibbled at the form.

We were forming quite a bond by this time, my horse and I. He never did much wrong, and if he would challenge me, it would be more mischievous than anything. The cloth that goes under the saddle is called the saddle cloth, or saddle towel. Basically, just a light cotton cloth, same as the numbered cloth the horses wore in the race. I would put it on his back, and he would reach back and pull it off when I was occupied with the saddle. He would look at me with such innocence when he did this. I would run my hand along his back to make sure he wasn't trying to tell me something, then try again.

He never kicked or bit, never pinned his ears back. He was just a kind little horse, and he was descended from a line that was legendary for a ferocious temperament. No one outside the stall thought I ever said a word, but I bet the horse wondered if I ever shut up. He was patient with me as I learned my way around a racehorse. He would lower his head for me when I put the bridle on him.

But as soon as I tightened the girth on the saddle, he stopped being a complete gentleman and turned into an impatient bully. You could tell by how many fresh wounds the stall had from being kicked what kind of bully you would have to deal with when you tightened the girth. It was going to be a challenge to keep him cooled out in the paddock before the race.

He had such alert, keen eyes. His personality was like his coat, understated, yet beautiful and elegant. Not a hair on him any color but dark brown, except the black hair on his mane, tail, and legs. By this time, he had rippling chest muscles, and powerful and muscular shoulders and hindquarters. He was a handful, but he was still a kind little horse. I was starting to get a little territorial as far as he was concerned.

Sunday morning, he was abusing the back stall, in danger of kicking a shoe off, injuring his foot or leg, or all of the above. Baldy sent me over to find Bux, to see if he was available to come by the barn. He said he'd be by in ten minutes, and he showed up then. Baldy said to Bux, "I just want to take him once around, real easy."

I wrapped Officer's Citation's front legs with polo wraps, to protect his lower legs and ankles from injury while in close contact with Bux's saddle horse.

I handed Bux the shank, and he led Officer's Citation to the gap and on to the track, walking past us at the rail. Baldy said to Bux, "Bring him in right away if he starts to get silly."

Bux nodded, and walked leisurely backtracking to the three-eighths pole, and then turned and led him at a slow gallop once around the track. Officer's Citation would kick at the moon once in a while, but he was feeling good, not getting worked up at all.

He was more relaxed when he came back, calmer after his morning jog.

I was starting to wash out a little bit, though. The big day was finally here.

I remember, because it never changes, how long it takes for the hours leading up to the race take to go by. We jogged him, I gave him a bath and applied Hooflex to his hooves, letting it dry all the way before taking him from the wash rack to the walker, and only let him walk enough to get dry.

When a horse gets excited before a race, or nervous, he will work himself into a sweat. Wet spots on his shoulders and flanks will appear, along with a white lather between his legs and on his hips and shoulders as he heats up and his anxiety level rises. This is referred to as 'washing out.' This takes a lot out of a horse, and so it is very important to create an environment that keeps the horse calm.

Which meant that the best thing I could do for the horse after he came off the walker was stay away from him.

When I arrived in the morning, I pulled Officer's Citation's water bucket and hay net but gave him a half can of oats and a few swallows of water after breakfast. Once on the walker, I completely stripped the straw from his stall, and when he was ready to come in, his stall had no water, hay, grain, or straw for him to eat or drink. The fifth race was around three-thirty or four o'clock on Sunday, and we had to dry out his system.

The majority of trainers, even then, used a diuretic called Lasix to dry the horse's system out before racing, but we did it by a slower process. By letting him expel the fluids naturally, letting time do the work and gradually dehydrating the horse through the course of the day, we could mitigate the damage a diuretic could do.

Excess fluid in a horses system can cause them to bleed through the lungs, but I don't have enough knowledge about how to explain the mechanics of it. This is why the water bucket is pulled and the excess fluids in the system are dried up. It is said that Lasix will give a horse who is on it an advantage over one who is not, but I don't believe this is the case. In fact, it seems more likely to put the horse at a disadvantage long term. After the race, we could give the horse a drink and quickly re-hydrate him, while our Lasix prescribed foes were still losing fluids for a full day, or more, after the race. Our horse had his weight back on before his foe had stopped losing his.

It's just a theory, and unconventional in the modern racing world, but it seems logical. In any event, it was the reason we stripped the stall completely. I finished this and disappeared with my form to Barbara's Backstretch cafe.

Cross Firing

The break. This photo looks like it is from the 50's or 60's, starting from the half-mile chute

It was after nine, and the track had closed early like it did every Sunday, so that it could be prepared and ready for the parade to post at one o'clock. I thought about breakfast, but decided against it, superstition winning out over repetition. I was really tired of the Backstretch Scramble. The half order had taken us to race day, but it was time for a change.

I rode my motorcycle out to the truck stop, a couple of miles away, and ordered eggs benedict. It was a poor choice considering I really liked eggs benedict, but If the horse didn't win we would have to try something different, superstition being what it is. I ate slowly, which is to say rapidly but slow for me. I glanced at the racing form once again, to see if I could make Officer's Citation a winner in this race. Maybe I could just have eggs benedict at a different restaurant when it was time to gamble, I finally decided.

Or I could just stop being superstitious, but it seemed like that might bring bad luck.

It felt like I must have spent an hour and a half at breakfast, but the clock was taking its time and lollygagging like a construction laborer unmotivated by the prospect of unemployment. It had been thirty-five minutes.

I rode the Yamaha to the Stockyards Inn, a steakhouse, lounge, card room, and racetrackers hangout on the way back to the track. It was around ten, three hours to the first race, two hours to kill. I parked outside and walked in. A wide covered deck lead to the double oak front doors, and I walked down the hall past the payphone and restrooms on the left and restaurant seating area behind a wall of multi-paned windows on the right, about thirty feet to the stairwell down to the cardroom.

"Rizzuto been in?" I asked the bartender.

"Not yet, hon," came the reply. "You want a beer?"

I walked to the left, around the end of the bar and pulled up a stool. "Nah, it's too early for that," I said. "How 'bout just a coffee."

"Throw a shot of Bailey's in there if ya want," she said, this middle-aged bartender I didn't know, but suddenly my favorite.

"That's the spirit," I said.

"That is the spirit, yes indeed." She had a deep smoky voice you can only get by picking up a pack a day habit fairly early in life.

I giggled with her, sipped my Bailey's and coffee, and told her it needed two more shots. She free poured a nice measure, up and down twice, and returned the bottle to the shelf with a flourish.

About this time, Bill Rizzuto, my employer, walked in, on his way to the cardroom. He didn't go down the stairs though. He looked into the lounge and spotted me. He came over, sat next to me, slid a fifty dollar bill in my direction, but kept his finger on it. "You mind taking a load of oats to Fred Davis?" he said. "Truck's loaded and parked outside."

"Depends on whether or not you let go of that, I guess," I said, glancing at the fifty.

Bill took his finger off the bill, gave me a smack on the back with his hand, and headed for the cardroom. "Just leave the truck in the lot, I'll get the keys after the race. You gonna tout me?"

Asking, did I have a tip on a horse. I was surprised the fifty didn't stick to his fingers.

"Chief says no."

Bill giggled rapidly, a habit he had when he reached a conclusion about something he saw or heard. Except at the card table. He was a pretty good poker player. "No tout, or no chance?" he asked, as he disappeared down the stairs. I liked Bill, he was pretty good to work for. He paid well and was fairly liberal with the occasional bonus for tough duty.

"Yes," I replied to my bartender. "How much I owe you?"

"It's on me, Hon. Tell your dad I said hi."

"I'll do that. How you know my pedigree, anyway?"

"We keep track of the good ones," she said.

"I imagine the bad ones, too," I said. "What's your name?"

"Sonny, but they call me Hooker," she said. I didn't ask why.

"Good to meetcha," I said, off the stool and headed for the parking lot, glad to have something to do to kill some time. I was fifty dollars richer and none the worse for wear after the triple Bailey's and coffee, probably less alcohol than a dose of cough syrup. I made a note not to mention the hooker thing in front of Mom. They were always faithful to each other, my parents, but still. I tried to leave Hooker a five dollar tip, but she shot a look at me that said, don't even think about it. "I'm Cole," I said, reaching out to shake her hand.

"Your ID says Colin," said Hooker. "You named after the horse?"

"I'm starting to wonder," I said.

We'll get to that, I promise.

I headed for the flatbed Nissan loaded with a ton of oats. It sounds like a lot, but it was only thirty bags or so, and I could pull in right next to the hay shed, top off the barrels from the truck, and stack the remainder in about ten minutes on a busy day, but I had a couple of hours to kill. I pulled out of the parking lot and took a left on Trent Avenue, an arterial that ran through the industrial area and next to the main lines of both the Union Pacific and Burlington Northern Railroad tracks.

About a mile down the road, I could take a sharp left, abrupt as a switchback, past an ugly yellow Quonset hut that was Rizzuto's feed and straw storage warehouse, Lazy K Feeds the name on the checks that came on schedule and never bounced. Bill was what they called a "good pay" on the backstretch.

I hung the left, driving easy, not all that interested in picking up ten bags of oats from the pavement as traffic whizzed past on Trent Avenue. The road jogged to the right, crossed an old arched wooden bridge, up and down, spanning the railroad tracks, which ran the length of a gully about twelve feet deep. A series of lefts and rights, about two of each starting with a right after the bridge, and you were at the entrance to the backstretch barn area on Haven street.

I put the Nissan in first gear and idled into the barn area, Freddie's being the first barn on the left once you took a left past the machine shed next to the guard shack. The machine shed, filled with tractors and implements designed to cripple loose Thoroughbreds, extended about forty feet, forming the north part of the U that surrounded the courtyard in front of Freddie's shed row, and the bottom of the U had a couple more stalls against the fence that separated the courtyard from Haven street.

In the center of the courtyard was Freddie's hot walker, the plywood motor curtains painted in the black and red colors of Freddie's racing silks. The bottom stall doors all along the shedrow, I think ten total, plus the two along the back fence, were painted black on the outside, the top painted black with a red sash running diagonally on the inside of the door, so that when the top door was open, as they always were, it was a checkerboard of black, with a red sash pointing down toward the horse. There was a white F on the top side of the sash, a white D on the bottom side. They were trimmed in red, the top doors. There were red and white bulbs and flowers decorating the borders of the courtyard and the hay shed, which was facing the first stall on the end of the barn next to the paved road through the barnyard. The wash rack was on the east side of the hayshed. A little bit of healthy green grass completed the picture. Freddie had a nice, private set-up, the hayshed obscuring some of the view of the courtyard.

Freddie was a character too, and kind of a buddy of Marv and Baldy. He had a fast and loud way of talking and had opinions that he wasn't afraid to share. He wasn't belligerent by any means, he just told it like it was as Fred Davis saw it. He was there when I pulled up to the shed. "Hey, Putzier!" he said to me as I idled up to the opening between the tack room and the hay shed.

"How you doin', Freddie?" I said, "Okay if I back in?"

"You got the whole ton?" he asked. "That fuckin' Rizzuto, he don't screw around, does he?"

Freddie had an unidentifiable accent, kind of midwest New England, with a dash of Texas. He thought and talked fast, and if he didn't drop an F-bomb twenty or more times during the conversation, you weren't talking to Freddie Davis. No relation to Keith Davis and they both got irritated if you asked. I backed in close to the hay shed, got out, and walked over to stand beside Freddie, behind the flatbed.

Freddie was about to tell me something I didn't know but sounded like truth when I heard it.

"Your old man come up to me once back when he had that horse Careless Ruler," Freddie said, "and he's wearin' that cowboy hat cocked off to the side like he does, and he says, 'Hey Freddie, I need a twenty dollar bill 'til Friday if you can swing it,' so I says to myself, this fuckin' cowboy's a good pay an' everybody knows it, so I says 'fuck yeah, Marv, anything you need.' " Freddie continued, "He says to me again, 'I'll catch ya Friday, an I says goddamnit, I ain't worried about it at the fuck all, you know?"

I was nodding along, laughing a little, enjoying the storytelling, not sure where the story was going.

"So Friday come, an' Marv an' Baldy got one in that day, that Careless Ruler sonofabitch, an' sure enough, here come the cowboy, your dad, reach into his shirt pocket like he does, pulls out that fuckin' twenty dollar bill, an' he says to me, 'We got that fuckin' horse in today, Freddie, I think he's gonna be a price,' and he hands me that fuckin' twenty an' he says, 'might be worth a bet', so I don't give a fuck, I go to the winda, bet that twenty on his fuckin' nose, and I'll be a sonofabitch if that fucker don't go off at twenty to one an' win that fuckin' race for fun." Freddie paused and shook his head, said, "Best God damn twenty dollars I ever invested, I mean to tell you."

"I liked old Careless, he's about the only one I remember from the old days, other than Reigh of Gold and Uneasy Edward," I said, still laughing. "Blackie, Goldie, and Ruler.

"That black sonofabitch," Freddie said, referring to Uneasy Edward. "He was a different fuckin' story." He continued, "You ain't gonna be nowhere today, but I bet they cash one on that little brown sonofabitch next out."

"Thanks, Freddie," I said. "I better get busy."

"Otherwise that fuckin' feed bill will be here before you get the truck unloaded." Freddie locked his tack room and headed toward the cafe. "Tell that god damned Rizzuto I don't want the hay 'til tomorrow."

"You got it."

Where else would you rather be today?

117

So I topped off Freddie's grain barrels, and stacked the rest of the oats on the pallet that kept them off the ground. I put the older bags on top, collected the empty bags and pulled out, turned right twice and exited the barn area. I parked the flatbed in the lot across the street, then started it again and headed back to the Stockyards to get my Yamaha, not wanting to leave it in the parking lot.

It was barely eleven, but there and back would kill a little time, and then I was going to the track, only five hours to post time. If nothing else, I could sit in the deserted guinea stand and listen to the clock slowly tick the seconds away.

Which is what I must have done, giving the horse a swallow of water around noon, the temperature around eighty degrees or so. I don't recall much happening until it was finally time to start getting Officer's Citation ready for his race.

By this time, Marv was in town, driving down with my mother, Carol, from the town of Tonasket, near the Canadian border in north central Washington. It was about a three-hour drive for me, two for my brother, and four for my dad, from the same house to the track.

Marv and Deke were at the stall, and Deke picked and cleaned Officer's Citations feet. I wiped the horse down with a damp cloth and put his bridle on. No wraps, no blinkers, no tongue tie, no frills.

Baldy always said, "If you don't know what the hell you're doing, just hang some more shit on their head."

Marv showed me how to lead the horse with the reins buckled together, one finger in between, and "Put 'em over his head slick and easy as you head him out in the stall."

Marv was the trainer listed in the program, and as such, would saddle him in the paddock. I heard the call, "Attention horsemen, bring your horses to the receiving barn for the fifth race. Horses to the receiving barn for the fifth race."

My heart leaped into my throat, and Marv said, "wait."

Baldy got up and shuffled toward the gate. "I'll see you over there," he said. "Don't get lost on the way to the receiving barn, Bass."

He was joking, but it was exactly what I feared the most.

By this time, a horse or two was coming toward the gap, headed for the receiving barn, the competition strolled past, and my horse calmly watched them walk by. "You know where the receiving barn is, Bass?" Marv asked me.

I made a non-committal noise, figuring I could just follow the horse that just walked by. "Just follow that shitter a Butterfield's, you'll find it," he said, pointing to the good looking chestnut walking past the barn. "Whaddya say, Darrell?"

"Good luck, Marv," said Darrell Butterfield, another pretty good friend of the brothers. "You gonna be anywhere?"

"Nah, prob'ly gonna need this one," My father replied. "Little red shitter oughta be tough, though," he said, nodding toward Darrell's horse.

"Look like we got a shot," said Darrell as he came over to shoot the bull with Marv, standing back and admiring Officer's Citation as he came out of the stall. "Jesus, he's a looker, ain't he?" he said as I came out of the stall and turned left, headed for the receiving barn with my horse.

Deke walked with me, and we headed past the gap, not really speaking, both of us a little washy, the horse coming up on his toes a little, walking faster as we got closer to the receiving barn.

The receiving barn was in the same place as the test barn but separated in some way that I don't recall. Which is strange, because I went to the receiving barn ten times that year, eleven if you count picking up the bridle. We went to the test barn every time he ran first or second, which he did five times out of ten tries.

But anyway, I didn't have to know where the test barn was for another couple of weeks. I walked him slowly around the ring, and the official at the receiving barn handed Deke the headstall number Officer's Citation would wear, number six. We heard the finish of the fourth, and then the announcement, "Attention horsemen, bring your horses to the paddock for the fifth race. Horses to the paddock for the fifth race."

I held Officer's Citations head while Deke slipped the headstall number on. The horses came out of their assigned stalls in order, one followed by two and three, four, five, and then me, feeling my heart once again trying to climb into my throat. Marv met us just outside as we led our horses around the north end of the track to the six and a half furlong chute. We turned left into the homestretch and headed for the paddock, where Marv would saddle the horse.

It was mid-afternoon, probably three forty-five or so. We walked along the outside rail of the track, some of the horses from the previous race coming back through the chute to the stable area behind the far turn, blowing hard, lathered up, with a kind of wide-eyed look of bewilderment in their eyes. These horses had run third or worse, no pictures or testing necessary, headed back to the barn for a bath and a freshly bedded stall.

As we turned right and went through the gap in the rail to the paddock, we went to the left and walked our horses around the oval-shaped path, clockwise. There was green grass in the center of the paddock, on which rested a statue of the northwest racing legend Turbulator. Marv and Baldy had tried to claim

Turbulator in 1970, but Turbulator stayed in his original barn, and Marv and Baldy went forward without him.

Apparently, the race was on the first day of the meet, and you had to have had a horse who had started at the meet to put a claim forth in Turbulator's race. They tried to buy a horse that ran in the first race after the race, but the owner wouldn't sell, as he couldn't figure out why they wanted his horse, felt like something was off. Marv said, when the trainer found out why they wanted the horse, he said, "If I had known what you boys were up to, I would have sold you the horse." Marv shook his head and tsk-tsk'd every time he told the story.

"Give him a turn and bring him in soon's the valet gets to the stall," Marv said.

I walked him around, as far to the outside of the ring as I could get, having the fastest walker in the ring, and maybe the toughest one to walk. About three-quarters of the others were walking with a lip chain, their heads bowed and looking down as the chain reminded them that pain was but a flick of the wrist away.

Baldy and Marv avoided the lip chain, believing it was easier to get the horse to relax without it, trusting the rest of it to the groom being able to handle the horse.

Now you've known them a few months, which would you rather do, try to control a hot blooded half-ton animal hopped up on iron supplements and B vitamins, or face the wrath of Marv and Baldy if you couldn't?

Officer's Citation was working me over pretty good, but it stopped me from washing out and started me sweating from the workout. I leaned against his shoulder as he pushed me around the walking ring, the valet finally coming from the jock's room with the saddle, waiting with Marv and Deke as I headed to the saddling stall.

The paddock judge, Bob Lightfoot, met us in front of the stall, lifted Officer's Citations upper lip, checked the tattoo a racehorse gets at the track before he makes his maiden start, looked at his paperwork and said, "Looks good, Marv."

"Head him out, Bass," Marv said, pointing his finger toward the ground and drawing a circle in the air. I went in head first, turning the horse toward me and slipping the reins over his head as he made the turn. Marv gave me a quick nod, and as the valet, on the right side of the horse, placed the saddle towel on the horses back, Marv helped straighten and move it forward so the back of the cloth was a couple of inches forward of the loin, covering about half back and half neck. The valet quickly and smoothly placed the saddle pad high on the withers, the front of the pad nearly straight above the front legs.

They folded the saddle cloth back over the top of the pad quickly and in perfect unison, about five seconds all the longer it had taken so far. The valet placed the saddle over the pad, still well forward, and placed his left hand on top of the saddle and stretched the girth belt under the horse, holding on until Marv had it, stretching it out under the horse and bringing the leather end through the front buckle on the saddle. While this is going on, I'm working the bit back and forth in Officer's Citations mouth, gently as possible, but actually leaning into him as he popped a sweat and came all the way up on his toes, as close to raising hell as he ever got in the paddock.

Marv got the first one buckled, and the valet straightened himself out, turning sideways during the procedure, wary of the girth slipping out of Marv's hand and smacking the family jewels nine times out of ten. Marv buckled the other strap, and the valet tightened his side. Marv cinched his side to the top hole, and the valet handed the overgirth, a four-inch elastic belt, over the top of the horse. Marv brought it up and over, down under, through the buckle, the valet was stretching toward Marv, the valet turning sideways again, Marv feeding the strap through and handing it back, up through the buckle, the valet cinching it up tight.

"Cut 'em in half and take another notch," Marv said to the valet.

"Good luck," the valet said, quickly moving to his second horse. the whole procedure had taken thirty seconds, and we were on the move as Marv tucked the belt into its keeper. "Give him a turn or two, Bass, keep your eye on me," he said. "Sell that sonofabitch," he said, gesturing toward the walking ring.

I looked to the right coming out, and the coast was clear, but we were coming out, regardless. I had a handful of Thoroughbred, and he knew why we were here, even if it was all new to me from this perspective. I took him in a wide circle, walking as slow as I could, trying to keep my horse calm without doing anything to make him burn energy. He was losing enough from nerves, damp spots appearing near his flanks, foam developing between his hind legs as he bounced around the walking ring.

Finally the Jockeys came out, Marv drew a circle in the air, and I went around again, holding the headstall with my left hand near the bit, my right over his neck, my hand on the rein on the off side.

We were on the side of the paddock opposite the stall when the paddock judge said, "Put your horses in."

Marv said, "Take a turn or two, keep him moving as we leg up."

"Riders up." My heart hit my throat again as the bugler played

123

the call to post. "Number one." I took another turn, trying not to turn him too tight, "two. Three, come on Terry, four!" Lightfoot said "five," then pointed at me, gave me a nod, and said, "six."

"Keep him moving, Bass," Marv said, as I watched in front, Officer's Citation jumped forward as Colton landed softly in the saddle, his feet dangling as we skipped forward. He tied the reins into a knot, and kept his legs out of the irons as I led him on to the track, Bux there to take him to the starting gate.

Bux handed me a leather strap as I approached, said "Through the D," and I slipped the strap through the opening where the headstall attached to the bit, put the ends together and handed it back to Bux. He nodded and led the horse forward, as I backed out of the space between the horses. I skipped behind my horse, staying alert, going to the rail, getting out of the way as the seven-horse repeated the procedure.

I met Deke, and he said, "We probably got time to slam one." We headed to the snake pit for a beer. I bet five dollars across the board, and we headed for the grandstand to get a better view, but ended up watching the race with Baldy at the bench in front of the concession stand, the monitor visible inside near the betting windows.

The horses paraded past the grandstand at a walk, one outrider in front of the procession and one behind. The first outrider pulled up and turned back to face the horses near the finish line, and the second stayed near the paddock.

The horses, after walking the length of the stretch, then make a U-turn, and gallop wrong way of the track to where the second outrider leads them, more or less in front of the guinea stand on the backstretch. They walk or jog as they warm up, usually following the jockey's direction, until the first outrider orders them into line by number. At about two minutes to post time, they begin making their way to the starting gate. The starting gate for a six-furlong race is about ten feet on the long side of the eighth pole on a five-furlong bullring, so we had a good view of them as Deke and I walked down and watched them load from behind the gate. We jogged to the bench, and turned to face the track as the announcer said, "They're all in line." It seems like forever when your horse is standing in the gate, but a moment later, the gates opened with a muted bang, the bell rang, and they were off.

"There they go."

I kissed my fifteen dollars goodbye before they crossed the finish line for the first time. The rider was standing in the irons and sawing the reins back and forth, pulling back, and running three wide into the turn, about five lengths behind the leader and falling back. He was about ten lengths out as they hit the quarter pole. He passed a few horses in the stretch but finished sixth in a ten horse field, about ten lengths behind the winner.

"Tsk," said Marv as he watched the horse run past the first time. Baldy gritted his teeth and shook his head pretty much the entire race. "That's called swinging," he said to me, motioning back and forth with his arms, imitating the jockey. "He gets back to the barn, I'll show you what cross firing means."

"Well, pick him up, and we'll see you back at the barn," Baldy said as he headed for the exit. Marv walked with us to the winner's circle, through it, and on to the track. Deke caught the horse as he came back after the race. He led Officer's Citation back to the walkway across the infield, and I walked beside him out in the middle of the track.

Marv walked back to the paddock with the jockey, but it didn't look like either of them had much to say. Baldy was just about to the pass-through gate, but Marv was confident he could catch him in the homestretch, Baldy not being much of a closer by the time July of 1987 rolled around. It didn't matter how loose on the lead he was, or how slow the pace.

We took our horse back to the wash rack, Deke holding him and trying to stay clean, me smelling like Epsom salt and horse sweat, Absorbine junior and shampoo, trying to get a truckload of sand out of the nooks and crannies of my horse. Deke watered him out while I bedded the stall.

We cut his feed back, filled the hay net and water bucket, and put a tired horse to bed that night. Marv and Carol came to the barn, and Marv said: "Do his legs up and cut him back a full gallon."

Officer's Citation stood still, patient while I put the mud on his legs, bandaged them, and wiped my hands with a paper towel. He had marks on his legs where his hooves had hit them because of the swinging, but other than that, he seemed ok.

Baldy said the horse was crossfiring and explained what it was. Cross firing is when the back hoof will strike the opposite front leg, and the front hoof will strike the opposite back leg, a result of the jockey swinging the horse's head back and forth. All parts function as one when a Thoroughbred is doing what he is designed to do, running. His legs follow his head, and when the head swings, the feet crossfire.

As I crawled under the top chain and snapped the bottom chain, the little horse walked forward, put his head in the feed tub, and began to eat.

"We're alright," said Marv, nudging me. "Boys, whaddya say we go get a snort over at the Flame, have some supper, and hash 'er out? I'll spring."

"Sounds good to me," I said. "See you there."

"Sure thing, Pops," said Deke.

Loose Horse

My Shyen at Bluegrass Dows in Paducah, Kentucky. Marcus Hartley is holding the horse, Randy D Crisler is the driver

The next morning, July 6, it was back to the routine, just me at the track and Baldy coming in later. The entire gang would have been there, but they suffered from the fate of being gainfully employed somewhere other than the backstretch.

I arrived at about six that morning. I am not, and have never been a morning person. The funny thing is, when I have a horse at the track, my eyes open in the morning, I blink twice and hop out of bed, thinking, "I get to go to the track today."

Years after this experience, I found myself in Paducah, Kentucky, photographing trotters and pacers, and learning the difference between the two. Trotting is a single gait, all legs working individually, while pacers move both legs on the same side at the same time. One of the trainers pointed out that pacers were easier, as they came by it naturally.

If you ever get the chance, pull up youtube videos of a pacer named Wiggle It Jiggle It. You won't regret it. You will also find Always B Miki. You will see Affirmed and Alydar in those two pacers if you are fortunate enough to have seen the battles between the two pairs of racehorses. To me, it boils down to three things; the horse, the track, and the racer. I saw those two pacers and realized I was addicted to racehorses as much as I was addicted to Thoroughbreds.

Every time I captured a photo of a racehorse raising hell in the winner's circle, that is the picture everyone who knows the racehorse wants.

I took a picture of a pacer named My Shyen at Bluegrass Downs In Paducah. Eighteen hundred miles from my home, and a long ways from a Thoroughbred or Quarter horse track, the trainer said the same thing they say up in the northwest when I asked her the question. I showed her the picture of the horse rearing on it's hind legs and asked, "You want this one?

"Yes," she said, "Hell yes."

Racehorses.

I was taking the photographs, not making enough money to even begin to pay for my associated expenses, but every day, thirty in all over the course of two years, I would wake up and say, "Someone is actually going to pay me to take pictures at the track today."

While I wish they would pay me more, I would do it free if I could swing it. I'm not a good enough photographer to demand more. I get to go to the track, and not only do I get paid, but I also get free admission and a free program. Sometimes, a half dozen free hotdogs after the last race from the concession stand. I don't abuse this perk, though. You ever ask yourself just what is in that hotdog?

It was all systems go with Officer's Citation, as far as I could tell. I would have to rinse the mud off his legs and wait until tomorrow to know for sure, but he cleaned up his feed and was demanding more. He didn't damage any snaps, but the guy at the feed store had better stay in stock if this is how the horse came back a day after the race.

I filled his water bucket, tossed him a can of oats, and headed to the guinea stand for an hours worth of therapy before I had to meet Baldy at the cafe. I would sit by the door, and it had two big sliding windows in front, always open on nice days. I could hear the horsemen and women at the rail, in the guinea stand, and on horseback in front of me.

Sometimes I would find myself involved in a conversation with a total stranger, feeling that we had many common bonds as we talked horses and racing. I would sometimes discover later that my new acquaintance was in a substantially higher income bracket, and the only common bond we had wasn't horse racing, so much as it was humility. Most of the time, I would just listen. It was like listening to a symphony of language, profanity bordering on sublime, cynicism blended with optimism.

So it was active that day, horses jogging by, wrong way against the outside rail, eight or ten people in the guinea stand, just as many on the rail, watching a horse, looking for a rider. I was probably the only loafer in the crowd. Don't ever let anyone tell you a one-horse stable is a bad thing.

"Bobby," says a trainer in the guinea stand, to a gallop boy jogging by on a horse.

"Whatcha got, boss?"

"Lope one for me?"

"Two after."

The trainer exits, having just arranged for the exercise rider to gallop a horse for him, probably a few minutes before nine. For the rider, it will be the second horse he rides after the break.

"What the…," a trainer stares intently, focusing somewhere on the far side of the track. His voice is soft, the questions he asks are only to himself, but he shares them with all of us, and soon I too am wondering, just what in the world is going on with that horse and rider. I can't quite see what horse he is watching, but I think it is the bad actor on the far side, near the grandstand.

"What are…you? What is he doing out there?"

That one actually was for all of us, but we don't know. No opinions offered, just a few tsk's.

"Loose horse, attention on the track, loose horse on the backstretch," spits the PA system. "Track is closed."

"Watch out, watch out, ok. ok. good."

So it wasn't his horse, but everything seems better and worse at the same time. We were holding our breath, wary of the havoc a loose horse on the track during training hours can cause. Racehorses are trained to run on the track, and it is what they do when they get loose. Horses do not see straight in front of them. They are built to swing their head from side to side in order to watch for predators from all points of the compass. Their defense mechanism is flight. They are not built to walk, they are built to run. See danger run, is the thought process of a wild horse. Otherwise, eat and drink. That's it. Those are the instincts. They could run into another horse head on, and never see them coming.

To help mitigate the threat of a loose horse, there are what are called outriders, usually two covering the entire track. They are the lifeguards of the track, of lives both human and horse. It is their duty to catch any loose horse on the track. The situation, as soon as the rider hits the ground and the horse begins running, becomes explosive. The horse is the fuse, and the fuse is lit. The bomb is hidden somewhere directly ahead of the horse, and the horse is not going to miss it. It is the job of the outrider to snuff the fuse as quickly as possible. The added challenge is the well being of the loose horse, whose well being is suddenly the lowest priority of any horse on the track.

"Heads up, loose horse, clubhouse turn." Speakers are broadcasting all around the track, everyone trying to spot the danger and not be the bomb. An ambulance is manned and ready to roll at all times during training hours. People and animals die in situations that start just like this.

Meanwhile, the outrider, on a big retired Thoroughbred, or a good Quarter horse, coming out of the half-mile chute, will pace the horse. A slow gallop at first, and then, bam! A burst of speed, and he's got the runaway crowded against the rail. He reaches down and grabs the rein with his left hand, from the wrong side, riding a good horse and earning every penny of his pay in that left-handed pick-up. Everyone in the guinea stand lets out their breath, along with everyone at the rail.

They gallop in unison, the outrider and the recently captured horse gradually pulling up past the gap, no damage done.

"Track is open for training, Track is open," comes the announcement, and we get back to business on every turn of the

132

evil oval.

You have to be at least part cowboy to be a good outrider. They are worth their horse's weight in gold.

I know you are anxious to get on with the training, and on to the races. So am I, but I guess we have to be patient like we had to then. The sights, the sounds, the smells, it was all just as much of a part of the experience as training the horse and learning the business. It was a fun place to be. I would stand at the rail, much more aware of everything around me than I ever realised at the time.

The sound a hoof makes when it strikes another hoof. The sound the water makes as it hits the dirt when the water truck drives by, high revs and low gear, shifting and gaining speed as it drives past. The tractors pulling the harrows, always one near and one far, the two of them making two circuits each, every training day and every race. The smells that come with all of these things. The smell of diesel smoke and desperation mingling near the finish line, where the two dollar bettors decide on a show ticket, while the bridge jumpers two hundred dollars in the hole are throwing good money after bad, looking for a monster at a price.

They would have one to bet on in a few days if they were lucky enough to see it coming.

It's like I'm writing about nothing that mattered, but every-thing did. I can hear the pop of a whip striking leather, and I can see a bay horse with a white blaze on his face, pinning his ears and looking back, leaping forward as he backtracks along the rail, a rider wearing a green helmet standing in the irons and pulling back. The more I do remember, the more I realize how all that didn't matter was everything that did. It was the only time in my life I was ever totally immersed in one world.

I had no outside interests when I was at the racetrack. Not to mention, I had a job that gave me total access to every room but the clubhouse, and at no charge.

As I sit here straining to recall, I find myself listening to a chain reaction from the train tracks along Trent Avenue, ninety-nine bangs a split second apart, moving fast along the line, from crossing to crossing at least, coming from ninety-nine steel hitches banging against each other as the train begins to roll. The bells at the crossing ring in the distance as the arms come down, the horn blows, two long, one short, and one long, and I am transported back in time, into an old white truck, crossing the wooden bridge as the train runs below, taking a load of straw to the stable area. What happened to that innocent kid, I wonder.

It was a pretty uneventful couple of weeks at the barn. If we needed to get Officer's Citation out without over-working him, we would usually get Bux and take him without a rider. He was fit, there was no need to keep getting him fit. Now the trick was to keep him sound. He was a little sore from interfering, cross firing. Sometimes it is a problem to be, hopefully, corrected by the farrier, but in our case, it was likely the rider swinging him the first time past the grandstand in the race. A few extra days off, and he was a tiger again, looking better every day. He would go for a leisurely gallop of about a mile and a quarter, two times around, at least four days a week. He would tear the stall down if we didn't get him out often enough.

We entered him in a race on Wednesday, July 22, 1987, naming Vince Ward to ride, an apprentice jockey allowed five pounds.

In the program, an apprentice rider is denoted by an asterisk, and they are generally known as bug boys because of this.

Or bug girls, of course. A single bug denoted a five-pound apprentice, a double bug ten. Ten-pound apprentices are just starting. Five pounders keep their bug for a full year after winning ten races, and a ten pounder loses the second bug after ten wins or one year after his or her first win, whichever comes first.

Twenty four hours before the race is when you administer the Butazolidin, a common equine painkiller. If you declared that your horse was running on Bute, as it is commonly known, your horse had to come up positive if he was tested. I don't remember how many milligrams each tablet was, but we crushed three tablets and administered them by working a section of hose down his throat, and then blowing into the hose and forcing the powder out. Similar to taking two aspirin before a football game, is how I thought of it.

It sounds somewhat crude and painful, but it was usually a fair fight between Officer's Citation and I. One night, he coughed as I blew, and I don't know how he felt, but I probably could have run a quarter in twenty-two and change that night. Not July 21st, though. Everything went well, and the next big day was but a revolution of the earth away.

I was at the track by six am. Baldy had reminded me the previous evening to get to the track early, pull the water bucket and strip the stall, and he arrived at his normal time. I had things pretty well in order when Baldy showed up with my cousin Guy. Guy was a few months younger than me, six inches taller, and a hundred thirty pounds heavier.

He was an all-conference defensive lineman playing for the University of Oregon at the time, and in the summer of 1987 was between his junior and senior years. He was, in the words of one of my more colorful friends, "Big as a house and pissed off all the time." It was partly true. He was a schoolyard bully, usually relaxed and on the muscle. Guy was tacking nearly three hundred pounds, had a low body fat percentage, and had been an avid weight lifter since about eighth grade. He embraced steroids wholeheartedly once he got to Eugene, which was like pouring gasoline on the fire of his already volatile personality. He liked to fight and was good at it. When Guy came to town, an assortment of drugs came with him, and trouble wasn't usually far behind. It was best to avoid him, if possible, but when he was around, he was hard to miss.

I don't know if it was just a habit from pacing Baldy, but like any world-class athlete, Guy's walk was a maddeningly slow strut. I noticed this phenomenon as my working career progressed, finally determining that athletes weren't cut out for construction work. None of them were worth a damn after the first break, two hours into the shift, and they were always walking slow, even though they could usually run pretty fast.

So Baldy came shuffling to the barn, Guy strolling casually along beside him, people coming out of the woodwork to greet the local star. Guy had an affable personality, was popular with the people at the track, and a fan favorite at Oregon. Baldy almost completely lost focus when Guy was around, and pretty much let him have his way no matter the situation. The first thing Guy did was walk up to the stall, grab Officer's Citation's head, and push it roughly aside, so he could look at the rest of the horse. We didn't quite have the same way of going around animals, Guy and I.

Years later, he was going to start a breeding operation with his NFL concussion settlement money. He'd never heard of Tesio and wasn't that interested in learning. Why would he need to know anything about the guy who permanently reshaped the breed, the man who could trace progeny from his stallion to half, maybe more, of all the Thoroughbreds currently competing in North America? I was surprised he wasn't more curious about Tesio. Tesio's unorthodox methods would have appealed to Guy.

He wanted to train Thoroughbreds with a rickshaw, the bike that the trotters and pacers pull. The theory, not a bad one, was about keeping weight off the horse. At the time we talked about this, I had been photographing the Standardbreds for a couple of years.

"I can see about thirty different accidents waiting to happen, breaking a hot-blooded two-year-old to the harness," I said. "Whaddya gonna do when they run off?

Guy said, "Just put a good brake on the cart."

"Yeah, but those bikes are pretty light. I'm not sure a brake would do anything." I didn't know much about training with a rickshaw. I'm not sure he did either.

"I could stop 'em," Guy said.

"All I know is, I watched one of the pacers run off with a veteran driver, and he had his hands full for at least three-quarters of a mile," I said, "Seems kind of high risk to me."

"Nah," Guy said.

I dropped the subject. Not much had changed in twenty-five years, and not much ever would by the time the Grim Reaper showed up at Guy's doorstep a few years later. He could be fun to be around, and he could make you wish you'd never met him. It just depended on his frame of mind.

I was happy for Guy's success on the football field. He pretty much ended up with the career I dreamed about, even ended up being taken under the wing of Mean Joe Green, the sole reason I was a Pittsburgh Steeler fan, and still am. When I was seven years old, I heard the name Mean Joe Green for the first time and decided that if there was a guy whose first name was Mean Joe on the field, he had to be on my team.

Guy sort of Forrest Gumped his way through that one, the Steelers putting him on waivers when a handgun was discovered in his room at training camp. This happened after he had served a thirty-day suspension for steroids. Yes, it was his gun. It was Baldy's gun, actually, and was probably less dangerous in Baldy's shaky left hand than it was in either of Guy's hands in those days. Either way, the Steelers were done with him. But when he was released by the Steelers, he ended up with a 49ers team that only lost one game on the way to a championship, so it all worked out. The one game they lost was to the Steelers, in case you were wondering.

Since brute force was usually his first option, I didn't care much for him being around the horse. Most of the horsemen liked Guy. He was funny, intelligent, and lived life at full speed. The truth is, I'd have skipped this entire introduction if he weren't so prominent that day. It was a day that created some interesting and irritating family dynamics for me, to put it mildly. His actions on July 22nd, 1987, had a surprising ripple effect in my future. It took a while for me to connect the dots, but that is how it all played out. It's quite a way to remember the day I broke my maiden at the racetrack. I usually tried to just mind my own business and stay out of the cross-fire when he was around.

So we went back, I put the shank around Officer's Citations nose, and Bux took him out, once around easy. When they came back, I hosed Officer's Citation off, applied the Hooflex, put him away, and got the hell away from everybody.

I went to the little restaurant on Sprague Avenue, and I had eggs benedict. I had to go to work delivering feed. At least I had eight hours of work to keep me occupied until the first post, at 6:15 pm.

Winner's Circle

Pretty good looking horse, eh?

Finally, July 22, 1987, race day. I would have been to the warehouse at about 9:45, so I could load the Nissan with bags of grain for delivery, or the old Ford box truck with bales of straw or hay. If it was a full load of hay, Bill usually helped, but a few bales here and there, I would handle it myself.

It was better if I did it myself with the hay, but after one memorable, miserable trip to the farm, Bill was a little nervous about me handling the hay deliveries alone.

The reason for his trepidation was well founded, but he didn't understand the situation. If I was alone, I could go slower and stay out of the dust.

I've always had hay fever, a low-level allergy to pollen and certain kinds of green plants and grasses, dried or not. I was usually good around most types of hay if we kept the dust down.

One hot summer day, we drove out to Plummer, Idaho, to get a load of Timothy, grass hay with long stalks and a head about two inches long where the pollen and seeds lived.

We started loading, me on the stack throwing the bales in the truck, Bill stacking. When it was about half loaded, we both were taking every other bale and stacking it in the interior of the box truck together. It was very dusty, and even though we were wearing those little paper masks, I started to get congested, and my eyes were watering. I was beginning to have an allergic reaction. It started fast when it started and got worse quickly.

This was nothing new to me but was usually horrifying enough for my employers to try to keep me away from this situation. I could minimize the problems once I knew what to watch out for. This is the day that Timothy Hay not only appeared on the list for the first time but went straight to number one on the danger list, nosing out Ryegrass for the top spot.

By the time the truck was loaded, I couldn't breathe through my nose, I was wheezing pretty badly, and my eyes were almost completely swollen shut. I stripped to the waist and ran cold water from the hose over my head until I could blow a few gallons of snot out of my nose. My face looked like that of a hungover Sumo wrestler. I rinsed my shirt, got all the green off of it, put it back on still wet, and climbed into the passenger side of the truck.

Bill came up to the door.

"I was going to have you drive...ARE YOU OK?" he said, seeing what was happening for the first time.

"Id'th pine, dthid habbens." (It's fine, this happens.)

If cell phones had been widely available then, he would have called an ambulance before I could calm him down.

As it was, we drove back to Spokane, about sixty miles, as I held my head out the window like a dog.

"You need to go to the hospital," Bill said.

"Doe, hod chower ad dec-oh-jes." I said. (No, a hot shower and decongestant.)

"You sure?"

"Deth." (Yes)

He drove me home, and I survived. But it scared the hell out of him. It happened to me once a summer, and was usually good for an afternoon off, at least. I never thought much of it, it's just the way it was.

So, anyway, we did the hay deliveries together after that, if for no other reason than the boss thought I might die if we didn't.

The next morning though, I loaded the Nissan with the grain and vitamin deliveries and took the first of what was probably two loads over to the track. I didn't like to go in much before eleven, when all the horses were back in their stalls, and the only activity was the tractor buzzing back and forth between the parking lot across Haven street and the barn area, emptying the manure carts on the pile where they would load it on to semi-trailers and sell it as fertilizer.

The manure carts were about the length of a large construction dumpster, maybe twelve or fifteen feet long, with sides about thirty inches high and open on top, with wheels on the back. They had a two by twelve board for a ramp so you could push the wheelbarrow in and dump it as you cleaned stalls. When it was full, the tractor would hook on to the front and take it to the pile in the parking lot.

So the grain deliveries could go in order around the stable, or if it was urgent, you organized by priority. Or you could just count total sacks, throw that many on the truck, and just peel as you go. I had no system, It really depended on the priorities. I was usually done with grain by noon. I would skip lunch, and then do hay and straw deliveries until about three o'clock, an hour or two before feed time. I usually loaded the trucks for the next morning if I finished early, which pretty much gave me the morning to spend with my horse or Baldy until ten or so.

By now it was four o'clock. I had given Officer's Citation a swallow of water at noon and ignored him as he raised hell about not getting lunch. He had been a terror on the snaps, and it wouldn't surprise me if we went through a dozen in the week leading up to the race.

If anything, he looked twice as good as he did before his last race. I stayed away as much as I could, but I was done with work, and Bill met me in the cafe and advanced me a hundred dollars without me asking. Not saying so, but making sure I could bet if I wanted to.

"Whaddya think?" he asked.

"I don't know, but he seems good. I think he'll run all he can today."

"Think he'll outrun his form?" Bill said, asking if Officer's

Citation might run a better race than it looked like he was capable of running.

I shrugged my shoulders. I was trying not to get my hopes up, as bewildered as the horse seemed during his first race. And I really didn't know.

"Do what you want," he said, "but Baldy usually runs a tough horse second out. You might consider investing that hundred."

Way ahead of ya, boss, on these considerations, I didn't say. I made a non-committal noise, and said, "You need anything else today?"

"No, go have some fun," he said.

I said, "I promise," and headed back to the barn.

I passed Freddie Davis on the way to the barn, and he said, "Hey Putzier. What the hell's your first name, anyway?"

"Colin," I said, stopping to talk. I liked talking to Marv and Baldy's buddies. I didn't know many people my age, and the previous generation was a lot more interesting, anyway.

"They name you after the horse?" he asked, chuckling.

I told you we would get to this.

"I was told it was Colin Kelly, the fighter pilot."

"Bullshit," said Freddie, "That fuckin' Marv named you after the horse."

"I wonder," I said.

"You know who Colin is?" he asked. "Only Champion to ever retire undefeated."

"Yeah, I've heard." Once or twice from Marv, and every time I used the name on the backstretch. I had started to go by Cole after high school, so my name wasn't such a source of amusement, but everything changed at the track. They even knew how to pronounce it, oh, like oh, boy, and not ah, like ah, shit. Nothing I could do about Putzier and most of my buddies called me Putz. So, it was probably best to not be very sensitive when it came to names. I Always wondered what it would be like to go through life with a name like Bill Smith.

"Your middle name Kelly?"

"No, Dale," I said. "It's the only normal name I have."

"There you go," said Freddie. "Go get that fuckin' money tonight." He continued on to the cafe, satisfied that I was rightly named after a racehorse and not some fighter pilot.

I still don't know for sure.

I did learn that the best horse Joe Gottstein believed he ever saw run was Colin. Keep reading, you'll meet Joe later.

In the meantime, let's meet Colin.

Of all the great horses trained by the legendary James Rowe, undefeated Colin was the one he admired the most, stating the only words he wanted to be written on his headstone were "He trained Colin."

Foaled at James R. Keene's Castleton Stud near Lexington, Ky., Colin was from the third crop of Commando out of the English stakes winner Pastorella, by Springfield. Colin was named after an old English poem concerning "Poor Colin." It seemed appropriate considering Keene didn't think much of the horse because of an enlarged hock.

Keene, however, had been wrong before. He was also disdainful of Colin's grandsire, Domino, a fiery steed that exceeded expectations and proved to be one of the top racehorses of the 19th century. Keene quickly changed his mind about Colin when none of his other horses could keep pace with him during speed trials.

Rowe brought Colin to the races for the first time May 29, 1907, at Belmont Park in a five-furlong cavalry charge down the old straight course against 23 maidens. Colin broke on top and won by two lengths without asking. Two days later, on the same course at the same distance, Colin set a track record of 58 seconds flat in winning the $5,000-added National Stallion Stakes by three lengths.

On June 5, Colin made his third start in a week and had his only serious challenge as a 2-year-old. Carrying 125 pounds in the $5,000-added Eclipse Stakes, Colin, according to a contemporary report, "ran a remarkable race, set the pace and was under pressure practically from the start, stood punishment with unflinching courage and outstayed (Harry Payne Whitney's) Beaucoup in a rousing finish. Beaucoup is a good colt, challenged the winner early after going a furlong and ran stride for stride with him to the finish, but could not quite get up."

Colin received a break of 24 days before returning in the $25,000-added Great Trial Stakes at Sheepshead Bay. Carrying 129 pounds, Colin won easily without being extended. He continued to roll, winning in succession the Brighton Junior Stakes, Saratoga Special, Grand Union Hotel Stakes, Futurity Stakes (setting a stakes record of 1:11 for six furlongs), Flatbush Stakes (equaling the track record of 1:24 for seven furlongs), Produce Stakes (defeating Fair Play by five lengths), Matron Stakes (again defeating Fair Play) and Champagne Stakes (establishing a new American record of 1:23 flat for seven furlongs).

Fair Play was the sire of Man O' War.

After completing his 2-year-old season undefeated in 12 starts with earnings of $129,205, Colin was being hailed as "the best horse ever bred in America or raced here" by the Thoroughbred Record.

Colin's first start as a 3-year-old in 1908 was in the

$10,000-added Withers Stakes at one mile, which he won easily. He came out of the race lame, however, and was declared out of the following week's Belmont Stakes by various newspapers.

There were various reports concerning the severity of Colin's injury. They ranged from slight soreness to severely bowed tendons in both his forelimbs. Whatever his condition, it did not deter Keene and Rowe from entering the 1-mile Belmont. In heavy rain and dense fog, Colin emerged with a five-length lead heading into the final quarter mile.

According to the race report, jockey Joe Notter "shook his whip at Colin and the colt came away quickly, but near the end, he was eased up, Notter thinking the race was over, and this mistake almost cost him the race," the chart caller noted. "Fair Play ran a wonderfully game race and stood a long stretch drive in the most resolute fashion imaginable."

Colin prevailed by a head. Although he was criticized for misjudging the finish line, Notter said he rode to Rowe's instructions of using as little possible of Colin because of his suspicious tendons and the poor track conditions.

Later that June, Colin made his final career start, winning the 1¼-mile Tidal Stakes at Sheepshead Bay by two lengths for his 15th victory without a defeat.

Keene sent Colin to England to race in 1909 with trainer Sam Darling. Colin, however, suffered an injury and never raced again. He was retired to the Heath Stud at Newmarket. Colin sired 11 stakes winners, including On Watch and Jock, as well as Neddie, grandsire of Alsab.

Colin lived to the age of 27. He died in 1932 at Capt. Raymond Belmont's Belray Farm near Middleburg, Va.

In "The Great Ones," Kent Hollingsworth wrote: "Great horses have been beaten by mischance, racing luck, injury and lesser horses running the race of their lives. None of these, however, took Colin. He was unbeatable."

So maybe you've just heard the story of my name. I'm still not sure.

If my conversation with Freddie would have lasted three hours, we would be set. As it was, post time for our race would probably end up being somewhere around eight thirty. We were in the sixth.

I checked on my horse and gave him a tiny swallow of water, and that was all he would get until after the race. I went home, changed, and for some reason put on a pair of white gym shoes. My superstitious nature should have thought of that at the time, but it didn't. I went back to the track, arriving at about five, in time to watch Sunday's replays with Marv and Deke in the cafe. This took us to about six, and we headed to the rail to watch the post parade for the first race and may have made a bet or two in the guinea stand.

Even though you couldn't see the finish, I loved watching the races from the backstretch, standing by the guinea stand at the rail. You could hear the sounds so much better, the most distinctive being the sound of one hoof striking another, a loud popping noise. You could hear the jockeys talking to each other, yelling in fear, or anger, competing. You could see who was running easy, who was hustling, who had no chance, and who looked like a winner at the quarter pole. It is something to see, a deep closer winding up on the backstretch, beginning to sprint as the pace slows down in front of him.

A light drizzle had been happening on and off all day, and as we watched the races, we could see that the Flag Officer's were running well in what was becoming a sloppy track. A sloppy track is a muddy track that the bottom hasn't fallen out of yet.

By this time Guy and Baldy had arrived, along with my aunt Judy, but I don't recall Carol being around. After the third race, I began to get the horse ready, not very much to do. The horses for the fourth were in the paddock, the horses for the fifth were in the receiving barn, and as soon as the third was over, the next races on the card would cycle through one more time. The sun was starting to set, and we would be racing under the lights.

I brushed his mane and tail, and gently wiped his body with a damp cloth. He was staying cool and calm and seemed to me to be getting his mind ready for the race. He would heave a heavy sigh once in a while, and switch his tail, but he was acting good.

Officer's Citation put his head down for me and accepted the bit readily, and shook his head a little when it was on, like an athlete doing his final stretching before the big game.

By this time, the five of us were all near the stall. I was inside with the horse, finishing the preparations, and Marv, Deke, Guy, and Baldy were all just outside the door.

"Guy's gonna take him to the paddock," Baldy announced. "Bass, you can pick him up. Deke, I just don't have anything for you to do."

Oh, boy.

I mean, seriously.

Dad tsk'd, and Deke took off without saying a word, as it turns out, walking to the front side after the fourth.

They made the call to go to the receiving barn, and Guy grabbed the horse by the head and led him out of the stall, turned left and headed for the receiving barn.

"You want to ride over with us, Bass?" Baldy asked.

"No, I'll walk over with Ace." Ace is what Deke and I called Marv, because he always said, "Hey, Ace," where anyone else might say, "Hey buddy."

"Guy might need some help in the receiving barn," Baldy said. I bit my tongue, and Marv said, "We'll run by in a minute."

"Think about the horse, not the circus," Marv said to me on the way to the receiving barn.

I waited while Marv got the headstall number on, and we walked over around the outside of the far turn and went through the six and a half furlong chute after the fifth, a few minutes ahead of Guy and the rest of the horses in the sixth race.

In spite of the circus, it worked out ok for me before the race. Marv was talking to some of the other trainers by the paddock, and I found Deke and a seven and seven waiting for me. "Drink up," he said, and not much else.

I hammered the drink and went to the window to bet. I bet twenty dollars to win, place, and show, known as "across the board," total cost sixty dollars, and then bet a twenty dollar exacta box on Officer's Citation, and a horse named Track Officer, also sired by Flag officer. Humans with the same sire are half brothers, but horses are not, they are just by the same sire. Half brothers are out of the same mare, with different sires. It was muddy, and the Flag Officers could run mud.

An exacta is when you pick two horses, and they have to run first and second in the exact order you pick them to win the bet. If you bet it both ways, you collect if they are first and second in either order, and this is known as boxing your bet.

Officer's Citation was number four, and Track Officer was number ten. Get your money ready, I'm going to take you to the window with me. Don't make a bunch of bets and then screw around digging out your wallet at the window, there are a bunch of gamblers behind you anxious to lose the house, so be ready. Are you ready?

I approached the window as soon as the person in front of

me was finished screwing around with their money, and said, "Twenty across on number four, twenty dollar exacta box four-ten." The machine puked the ticket out, to borrow a turn of phrase from Marv, and the teller said, "Hundred, thank you, good luck." I paid with the hundred dollar bill that had been burning a hole in my pocket since Bill gave it to me a few hours ago.

I went back to the bar, signalled to the bartender, and bought two more drinks for Deke and I. It didn't help with washing out much, but a quick snort before the race became a long-standing tradition from then through the time when Deke sold his last Thoroughbred. The drinks were gone as soon as we got them, and we headed for the paddock rail to look at the horse.

It looked like Guy might make it through without punching the horse is all I'm going to say about the paddock. They saddled the horse, and legged the apprentice, Vince Ward, up and onto Officer's Citation's back.

Deke and I met Marv coming out of the paddock, and Guy must have gone to sit with Baldy and Judy on the bench in front of the concession stand. "Well, shall we get a snort?" Marv asked.

Deke and I were willing enough. I have no recollection of where they watched the race, but I was at the eighth pole, right in front of the starting gate for the six-furlong sprint, and the butterflies were churning in my stomach as the horses approached the gate. The light drizzle was back, not that I would have been aware at the time. The track was sloppy and about four inches deep, on the dry side of perfect for a Flag Officer.

I was standing an eighth of a mile from the finish line, which is just past the winner's circle. The winner's circle is where you access the track to pick up your horse after the race. I say that for future reference, about one minute from now.

"They're all in the gate," Racing Secretary and track announcer Norm Admunson said, over the loudspeaker.

My heart slammed into my throat.

A muted bang as the gates open, the bell rings, the announcer said, "There they go......Officer's Citation is away best, he'll have the early lead..." and the call continued, but I didn't hear any of the rest of it, I swear.

The butterflies start to go away and get worse all at the same time. You wonder if he can hang on, or will he collapse at the quarter pole like many a cheap speed horse before him? He was running easy though, into and down the backstretch with one horse beside him, past the guinea stand, fast approaching the quarter pole, around the turn still in front, starting to increase his lead as they turn left and enter the home stretch.

Approaching the eighth pole now, Officer's Citation's lead is just getting wider, little by little and nothing is running late. Next thing I know, I am sprinting down the tarmac beside my horse on the track. I don't know if Officer's Citation got the last eighth in twelve seconds or not, but I'm pretty sure I did.

We were an easy winner, and only after leaping up the steps to the winner's circle did I notice that Track Officer ran third, screwing up my exacta and costing me forty dollars. It didn't matter, though, because Officer's Citation's final odds were sixteen to one, and I would have every number on the Tote board times ten, except for the exacta, which probably paid a couple hundred for a two dollar bet.

As the horses pulled up and jogged back to the winner's circle, I was watching for the tote board to flash, even though I knew that they wouldn't make the race official until the last jockey weighed in, which would be Vince, after the picture.

I was waiting to pick up my horse when I was body-checked by an all-conference defensive lineman who was still trying hard to fuck up a perfect day.

"Who's picking up the horse?" I asked.

"I AM," said Guy, his face flushed.

Holy Jesus, Lord give me strength.

Guy was invisible when there was work to be done, but he was always available when there was glory to be had. I kind of felt sorry for the asshole, but not this night.

In the picture, you see a serious, disgusted version of Deke, a happy version of me wearing white Reeboks, and an overgrown manchild muscling the head of a damn good looking horse toward the camera.

"I think it looks good, the way I turned his head," Guy said after we saw the picture.

The photographer took the picture, the glory captured for all time, and Guy,who now held the horse with one hand, turned and said to me, "Hey Bass, you mind taking him to the test barn?"

I figured he'd want to be there for the accolades.

"Huh." An involuntary chuckle escaped, and I took hold of the reins, untied the knot, and slipped them over Officer's Citations head. I put my hand under the headstall on both sides and gave him a quick scratch, then headed for the pathway across the infield, Deke walking next to me. "You coming to the test barn?" I asked him.

"No," He said. "See you in time for the tri, or the Flame."

We usually split a trifecta on the last race, and sometimes we cashed.

"Okay," I said, and it was me and my horse, again. I gave

him a pat on the neck, and said to him, "Thirty-three ten times ten, times two for place and show. That's damned near seven hundred you made me today, and eight eighty for you."

In the meantime, I have an attractive young female following me to the test barn, but she was just doing her job, keeping the horse in sight from the time it crossed the wire until the urine specimen was collected. She had a long wait, I had a very dehydrated horse on my hands.

So I went to the test barn asking her for directions as we got to the gap. "It's that way," she said, pointing vaguely past the gap and to the left.

We made it, and there was a horse or two there, the first or second place horses all being tested, plus the occasional random test for horses who ran noticeably better or worse than their form indicated they would.

I held the horse and gave him a small drink, while two test barn employees shampooed him. I then snapped him to the hot walker, letting him walk, stopping the walker every few minutes to give him a small drink until his coat started to dry, and he gradually quenched his thirst. After about twenty-five or thirty minutes, he was done drinking, and we put him in a stall and stood there waiting for him to urinate.

Horses on Lasix are in and out of the test barn fairly quickly, as Lasix is intended to eliminate water through urination. On the other hand, Officer's Citation was bone dry, and was re-hydrated, but didn't have much excess liquid to expel. It was going to take a while and another bucket of water before I could take my horse back to the barn.

Marv and Deke came by after the ninth, and I was still waiting. The stall was bedded, the feed was ready, all they needed was the horse. Marv looked him over, said, "Looks like he came back all right, huh, Bass?"

"Seems good to me."

"Tap the till?"

"Seven hundred," I said.

"Jesus. You buying?"

"I was thinking prime rib over at the Stockyards."

"I don't know about prime rib, but I might eat a t-bone."

"Well, I'll buy it, whatever you do."

"Okay, pard," he said. "We'll see you back at the barn."

I was the second to last horse out of the test barn that night, the only time I ever beat another horse back to the stable in five trips to the test barn that year.

We went to the Stockyards Inn, and Marv bought the steaks, having tapped the till pretty good himself that evening.

Play Your Tension

A good looking brown Thoroughbred I photographed one morning at Presque Isle Downs in Erie, Pennsylvania.

One afternoon in the summer of 1987, Marv and I walked into the Stockyards Inn and found a table in the lounge. We sat down with our racing forms, and looked up as the waitress came over to the table.

"Hey, Ace," said Marv to the waitress.

Marv was good friends with the owner, Ted Stephens. In fact, it was Ted who bought Redda Rosa, the Thoroughbred I had cared for at home when I was about ten. He was the first Thoroughbred I remember more than vaguely, and the reason I had a savings account, two hundred and fifty dollars, ten percent of the sale price. Marv never paid the cover charge at the Stockyards, open tab if he wanted it. He didn't. Marv had a book on who was a good pay in all matters, up and up, and down low, and Ted was A-plus in that book.

Ted never said no to anything Marv asked, a regular before our waitress was born and ever since.

"Whatcha havin', cowboy?" she asked Marv, not knowing his drink. He probably thought she was new.

"Screwdriver," he said.

She turned to me. "How 'bout you, hon, Seven and Seven?"

"Nah," I said.

She said, "screwdriver?"

I shook my head. I had to go back to work later.

"Bud Light?"

"Not today," I said.

"Are you drinking Pepsi today? You gotta go back to work?"

I nodded.

"Ok, you two," she said. "Be right back."

I watched her walk off, not a bad view at all, and looked over at Marv. He was arching an eyebrow in my direction, lifting his brown felt cowboy hat just a little.

"Been here before, have ya, Bass?" He asked, more statement than question.

"First time ever," I said. "I think she's psychic."

"Look like it from here," he said, giving his head that one shake.

******

Officer's Citation came back better from the win than he had from his first race, without a mark on him. I didn't see any signs of a sore neck from the winner's circle experience, and no black eyes from the paddock, so he had come through with flying colors and survived the glory intact.

I'd like to say this was good for my ego, having a winner, but it was actually terrible. For a few weeks my ego was swollen quite a bit more than was healthy. The racing gods would take care of that soon enough. For now, however, I was pretty sure we were going to win seven or eight in a row, and cap it off with the two-miler in the late fall.

I was also pretty sure we were ready for stakes company, but Marv and Baldy insisted that he was just a cheap little bottom horse, still eligible for his never won three condition race. So okay, if we get that out of the way, then we could jump him up to the top rung from the bottom. After all, he was four by four to War Admiral, out of a Citation mare, and could trace the top side of his pedigree to Ribot, the perfect Thoroughbred specimen.

Marv and Baldy had actually been around good horses and knew the difference. It might have been a win at a good price in their second start since the early seventies, but they weren't inclined to swell up over a cheap condition horse.

The groom was a different story.

Officer's Citation cleaned up his feed, and his feet were cold, his knees were fine, absolutely nothing was wrong. The race didn't take much more out of him than a fast work would have. I was amazed at how easy this was.

What wasn't going to be easy was going back down to the farm for harvest in August. I had worked for the same family for about six years now, and they would have adopted me for the asking. I solved both issues by asking for one hundred dollars a day, up from seventy, and went from being a helluva young man to an arrogant asshole who couldn't do anything right.

It solved a couple of dilemmas, though, and it finally was a big step toward leaving the farm, and the Palouse, for good.

The first dilemma was how to be at the racetrack often. But this was actually resolved pretty well because harvest, normally a grueling marathon, got way easier for me. Instead of thirty-two sixteen hour days in a row, I worked twenty-two days with every weekend off. I was being punished by reduced days, but I would head for Spokane every Friday night and not go back to the farm until six o'clock Monday morning. The punishment was having to spend the entire weekend at the track instead of a hot, dusty, wheat field. I was happy to serve the time.

Rizzuto didn't want me to go in the first place, but I was committed. He had no idea how much dynamite I placed under the bridge to get weekends off in the first place. I helped Bill out whenever I could.

As soon as harvest ended, I collected my check and left Nelson Brothers Farms for the last time, stopping by for a visit just once in the next thirty years. I hadn't really thought about that until just now, but that's how it all threshed out. Nothing personal, it's just kind of an out of the way place.

I worked one more harvest the next year for a different farmer and had a hell of a good time. Turned out to be a good one to end it on. I think I got seventy dollars a day.

Looking back, I wouldn't have traded the experience for anything. These days, I don't mind driving through the Palouse country and remembering, but I've never had any inclination to go back for good. Good times they were.

We had one more race before that, though, coming back a week and a half after the win. We were running never won three for $4000 claiming, stretching out by a sixteenth of a mile to six and a half furlongs. To ask Officer's Citation to run against tougher horses was challenging enough without adding distance, but that is what we asked him to do.

We were in at six and a half furlongs on Saturday, August 1, 1987, in the tenth race. It would be the first of seven races where we were in the last race of the night, post time somewhere around ten pm.

Because we were usually in the nightcap and ran second four times that year, I got to spend quite a few extra hours with young ladies my own age in the test barn, but none of them ever seemed all that happy about it. My dehydrated little horse would keep us there until one o'clock in the morning sometimes. They all liked Officer's Citation, though. I thought about taking him for walks in the park, the way he attracted beautiful women.

The day before the race, a stall became available in the barn adjacent to us, two stalls from this end, same distance to everything but away from the track. We would not have to move anything but the horse and the stall chains, and they would probably be half torn down anyway.

Baldy said it was up to me whether we moved him or not, and I compounded his mistake in trusting me with the decision by making the wrong one. Not thinking of anything but the location, I said yes.

"You're sure?" he asked.

"Yeah." I couldn't figure out why he thought there was something to decide.

I don't know if it was supposed to be a lesson that stuck, but that's what it turned out to be.

I prepared the stall with screw eyes, one for the water bucket and three for the feed tub. I screwed in a screw eye attached to a larger ring up high so I could tie him in his stall, filled in the holes and leveled the ground in his stall, broke open a bale of straw and shook it out, transferred his water bucket and feed tub, and let him walk for a few minutes on the hot walker while I prepared his evening feed. I twisted six long shanked screw eyes into the wood framing of the door, three on each side. I had a zinc snap sandwiched by two brass snaps on each side of the top chain.

I put the feed in his tub, led him into his new stall, snapped one of the brass snaps across and onto the screw eye for safety, took his halter off and ended up with a sore back and damned near a loose horse.

He bolted for the door, and I hit him with a body block in the chest, enough to knock him off stride and keep him in the stall. The impact knocked me into the top chain, the only one I had snapped. He would have destroyed the brass snap, and I think we both knew it. I could testify that he was on the muscle.

I ducked under the chain, and from one knee, snapped the bottom chain, and then crawled over and draped myself over a straw bale. I was trying to stretch my back and catch my breath. I ended up with a cool looking chain shaped bruise across my lower back, but I really could have done without it.

My air slowly came back as I listened to sounds that don't come from a horse calmly eating his dinner.

161

"Play your tension around these Thoroughbreds, Bass."

I was getting tired of sudden and painful reminders to heed Marv's advice.

No, those sounds I was hearing are the type that come from a horse who is more than just a little agitated by his current situation. I pushed myself up and quickly laid back down. "Ouch," I said to myself.

Bang, went the foot of an irritated racehorse, striking the wall behind him.

"Make that crazy sonofabitch stop kicking," came a shrill voice from the other side of the wall.

"Huuurrrngn," was my reply.

"Oof," I said to myself, softly. The more it hurts, the quieter I get, usually.

The one exception was when I jumped into a bed of red hot coals when I was seven years old. I tried to jump over, but ended up jumping into the coal bed. I just thought it was a pile of ashes. I'm pretty sure I screamed. A week after I got the cast off my arm, this was. I didn't make a sound when I broke my arm, or when they set the bone. I didn't know I was supposed to cry, so I didn't.

Honestly, I didn't think I was allowed to cry.

Seven weeks after I broke my arm, on the way to the swimming pool for the first time all summer, we jump the ash pile, or almost. Next thing you know, I'm two months soaking my feet in ice water and vitamin E oil. It wasn't just the burns. We had to walk about a quarter mile home with severely burned feet, both of mine and one foot each for my two cohorts. They took turns carrying me for about twenty steps apiece. After that, I was on my own. Barefoot. On a gravel road. I cried loudly. A lot. Fire is ten on the pain scale, and nothing else compares.

It was a hell of a way for a seven-year-old to spend the summer. I healed up in time to walk to school on the first day of third grade, pleasing everyone, with the exception of myself. Damn near burn the skin off my feet, and I don't miss a single day of school. It wasn't fair.

But for all pain excepting fire, I took a cue from the horse and suffered in silence.

Blam! Turn a circle. Blam! Turn a circle, kick the wall. Blam! "Aaaaaugghh," I groaned softly.

Blam, kicked Officer's Citation, not very softly. Quick circle, bang! Squeal, Bla-blam. Two feet that time.

I could hear footsteps quickly approaching, "CAN YOU MAKE THAT... oh my god are you ok?"

"Hu-uh," I said, nodding my head. I raised my head, and she helped me up to my feet. I stretched my back, tentatively reaching for my toes. I was going to survive.

Blam!

"Hey, stop kicking," I said to my horse, barely audible, trying to touch my toes, stretch my back.

I looked at her, I didn't know exactly who it was. My new neighbor at the barn. "He doesn't understand," I said to her apologetically.

"He'll settle down," she said. "You ok?" Concern in her voice.

I coughed, "Yup," I said. "Thanks."

Blam!

She shot an irritated look at Officer's Citation's stall. "You go see a doctor if you spit up any blood." Not so softly this time, not much concern in her voice at all.

"Ok."

Blam!

Shit.

"Thanks," I wheezed.

The horse didn't seem very relaxed, but he was definitely on the muscle. I shut the top door on his stall, and the bottom, hoping the darkness would get him settled down and into the feed tub.

Blam!

I went to the cafe for a bowl of soup, two hours to kill before medication. I swear I could hear him blasting the wall from inside the cafe. I ate slowly and asked for a bag of ice if they could spare it. One of the waitresses iced my back and read the racing form with me for about fifteen minutes. She said she thought we had a chance. "In the race?" I asked.

"Yeah."

"Oh," I said, unenthusiastically.

She thumped me on my head with her wedding ring. "Better?" she asked.

"Little headache, but I think I'll make it," I said. "Thank you."

"Be careful, hon," she said. "You need some Motrin?"

I nodded, said, "Thanks," and headed for the door.

I walked back down to the barn and was getting my hopes up when I heard him blast the wall again.

This day had turned to shit in a hurry.

My horse was wringing wet as I ducked under the chains, moving slow and staying alert. I put a hand under his chin and led him to the feed tub, where he took a nervous bite. Then he went to the door, turned a circle and kicked the wall. But he took another bite, and then another as I rubbed his mane and neck.

I stayed in the stall for the next couple of hours with him, talking to him quietly, doing what I could to keep him calm.

Eventually, it was time to crush the Bute pills and get them down his throat.

I smeared a little Vaseline on the outside of the hose, got it down his throat, and blew the medication home. He spits the hose out and almost struck me as he stood on his hind legs, came down and kicked the back wall with both hind feet.

"Come on, now," I said. The sweat was dry now, you could see residue from the lather.

"Easy, baby," I said, rubbing his neck, rubbing his back where the hair had dried together.

Shit.

I think It was after midnight by the time he settled down. I gave him another pat on the neck, crawled gingerly under the chains, and headed out to see if I could get some sleep.

Blam! Said my horse, bidding me goodnight.

Shit.

I went home to soak in a hot bath, popped a few Tylenol and Motrin, and tried to sleep.

Blam! I thought as I kicked at the wall beside my bed.

******

The next morning, I wasn't up early, so much as I was still up. The welt across my back made it difficult enough to sleep, but I swear I could hear that little brown horse kicking the stall from five miles away. It was probably around seven when I was back at the cafe. I got a coffee and walked to the barn.

I never even thought of going to the old stall, which is surprising, considering what the routine had been for more than a hundred days. All the action had occurred in the new stall, however, and I turned left into the shedrow.

Blam!

Shit.

He'd left about a quart of feed in the bottom of the tub. His legs were warm from pacing the stall. His back feet were warm from kicking. He looked like I felt, bug-eyed and goofy. And it was race day.

I cleaned out his feed tub and rinsed and filled his water bucket about a quarter full.

I tossed him a can of oats.

He took a nervous bite of grain, went to the stall door and looked to the right.

Marv was standing in front of the old stall.

"When did you move over there?" he asked.

"Yesterday."

"Tsk." He shook his head, once. I was looking at the top of his white straw hat for just a second.

"I'm not sure I approve a that."

I didn't say anything, wishing I were somewhere else for the second to last time that year. A heavy silence hung in the air between us. I learned in the principal's office to not answer the questions that weren't asked. I'm not sure it was the proper tactic in this case, but I had no idea what to say.

The silence either invited further comment, or it didn't. Staying true to form, silence prevailed. For damned near fifteen minutes, and it seemed like an hour.

"He clean up?" Marv said, eventually, way quieter now.

"Left about a half a can, little less," I said.

"Tsk," he tsk'd.

"You want a coffee?" I asked.

"Yeah." Looking at me thoughtfully.

"You wanna walk up with me?"

"You hurt your back?"

"Let's go get a coffee," I said, finally letting out my breath.

We started walking toward the cafe, cutting through the shedrow. Don't do this if you don't have a horse in the shedrow. But we did. A tired, goofy horse who was racing in fifteen hours, was in this shedrow. You might have heard us move in, I think we might have made some noise.

Marv said, "What the hell happened, Bass?" Concerned. I was trying not to show it, but my back was killing me.

"I moved him to a new stall, is most of the story."

Blam!

Shit.

Marv looked at me and raised an eyebrow. The pissed off or damn close to it look. "Whose Idea was that?"

"Baldy said it was up to me, so that's what I did," I said, feeling something, felt a little bit like humility.

"Uh," he grunted, acknowledging, not offering an opinion, or any indication of his current state of mind. We walked a little further.

"The hell you do to your back?"

Mentally, I was a boxer leaning against the ropes and covering up, because whatever "it" turned out to be, it was coming. I may have been Baldy's accidental protege, but I was Marv's kid, and there was a certain amount of something that came with that. I was about to find out how far I came up short.

"The horse took a lunge at the door, and I was between him and it when we hit the chain."

He put the back of his left hand on the front of my right shoulder and applied a little pressure. We were now face to face, those gray-blue eyes piercing into mine from under the curved brim of that hat. "You pay attention around these Thoroughbreds, Bass," he said. "They don't cripple you, they'll kill you you don't, you hear?"

167

I nodded. "Yes."

He nodded once, and turned to go through the gate at the guard shack. I was behind him now, and caught up as he held the door open for me to enter the cafe. "I don't think there's a hell of a lot needs to be said about moving the stall the day before a race," he said. "Whaddya say we get some breakfast, wait for the Mouthpiece to show up?"

Baldy was going to law school at Gonzaga at the time, and so had acquired yet another nickname, The Mouthpiece.

Me, I was starting to realize I was getting to know a little bit more about this cowboy who raised me.

I ordered two eggs over easy, hashbrowns and wheat toast, not thinking too much about it. Marv had a couple of poached eggs.

We were drinking coffee and reading the form, handicapping the race when Baldy came in. I pulled a chair out for him across from Marv and had Baldy's coffee on the table as he sat down and looked around. I pulled up a chair beside him, and he asked, "How's your horse?"

"He's, uh..." I began.

"He's a little hot this morning," Marv said. "For some god damned reason."

The brothers each had an eyebrow arched a little as they looked at each other, and seemed to hold the look for a little longer than may have been usual.

Baldy gritted his teeth and nodded his head, just a little, but several times. "Get me a straw for my coffee, would you, Bass?" he said. "Throw a couple ice cubes in that son of a bitch."

Twitching Thumbs

Horses on the mechanical hot walker.

It wasn't the worst decision in the world. I had done it without thinking much about what the fallout would be, what we would have to change going forward. But the decision was made, the deed was done, and we would await the outcome of the race to see how we would proceed.

If we won, I would be stuck with two eggs, hash browns, and wheat toast for the rest of the meet. Even if we just hit the board, after all this, I would think about the power of hashbrowns and wheat toast. Fourth or worse, it was an open menu.

We would move forward, either way.

There is more to superstition than simply avoiding black cats.

We walked back to the new stall. Marv and I walked slowly as Baldy stomped and shuffled along between us, the best bad leg supporting the worst as he threw it forward, adjusted his aim, planted the bad leg, brought the good bad one forward, and then repeated the process. No one ever talked to him about a wheelchair, he wasn't interested, and he didn't get interested for more than a decade after that.

Baldy was a student of the racetrack. He noticed everything that went on, saw everything between the barn and the cafe, and the whole time appeared to watch the ground in front of him as he walked.

My earliest memory of Baldy was in the dining room of the house we lived in when I was born. We moved from that house to Endicott, in the Palouse country, Whitman County, Washington, the summer before my sixth birthday, so this had to be around 1971 or earlier.

In the dining room, there was a black rotary phone hanging on the wall, about five feet above the floor. If you were sitting at the table, you had to reach up to hang the phone in its cradle. I remember Baldy, the handset in his hand, reaching up, and slowly, inch by inch, as though it weighed two hundred pounds and he was pushing it up a hill, slowly lift that handset toward the cradle.

Marv glanced up, and quickly looked away.

I stood transfixed, as though nothing else on earth was happening at that moment. I couldn't have been more than four or five years old, but I remember it like it was yesterday, watching the steadiest unsteady hands I had ever seen, ever would see. I knew he moved differently than the cowboy, but I never saw him as weak. I hesitate to even say different. I think slower is the only word that ever came to mind.

He once stayed at our house, and I helped him get dressed in the morning.

"Does this bother you, Bass?" he asked.

"No," I said. "I would think it bothers you more than me."

"It does," he said. "The way you keep fucking it up is what bothers me most."

"You want to run around with your pants unzipped today?" I asked.

"Make things a hell of a lot easier," he said.

"Well, we can't have that," I said.

He looked down past his badly tucked shirt and said, "Zip that fucker up."

One day during that memorable summer of 1987, Baldy and I were sitting on his bench at the gap. I had said something as it pertains to life, from a viewpoint that was clearly influenced by both pedigree and environment, and he arched one of those eyebrows in my direction. He was smiling, his missing tooth that Marv had taken out with a slingshot many years before clearly visible. I had respect and admiration for the way Baldy's mind worked. He leaned toward me.

"Hey," he said, "watch out you ever get a twitch in your left thumb."

High praise indeed.

Blam! The sound of a shod hoof kicking a wall brought me back to the present day, and an agitated horse.

Baldy arched an eyebrow this way. I shook my head. He grinned, barely. More of a grimace, really. Then he gritted his teeth and shook his head.

"Tsk," Marv said, giving it that one shake.

We stood in front of the stall, and the horse started forward.

"Hey," said Baldy, in a low tone.

Officer's Citation stopped, pricked his ears.

They looked at each other for a long moment.

"Get him out, Bass," said Marv, with a little flick of a wrist from the stall to the walker. "Strip that stall."

"Check his shoes," Baldy said. "Son of a bitch prob'ly kicked one loose."

So I got a cotton lead rope, the leather shank, the mane card, my hoof pick, and a damp cotton rag. I unsnapped the bottom chain after taking his halter off the hook outside his stall. I crawled inside the stall gingerly, and Officer's Citation hadn't moved from where Baldy stopped him.

"Whoa baby," I said softly. I dropped the shank and the tools in his feed tub, his oats lying there, barely disturbed. "Easy now."

I put the halter and shank in his feed tub, my hands empty now, and stepped over to him, my left hand reaching up to stroke his neck on the off side. He began to rub his head against me, itching from the dried sweat. I moved around him slowly, rubbing his chest, his back, his hindquarters, his ribcage, working from front to back, around, and back to front again, and when I got to his head, he rubbed the other side against my hand. I stood in front of him and held my hand steady while he moves his head up and down, doing the work himself.

I don't know why I did it this way. I felt like it was what he was asking me to do. Like he was saying that if I looked closer, maybe the lessons would be easier. I was beginning to figure out that he was trying to talk to me, but I couldn't speak his language. I was at his chest now, his head behind me, and he reached down and nuzzled me on my back, where the bruise was, breathing on it, the hot breath of this Thoroughbred caressing the bruise, barely touching it. Telling me, "pay attention, or I will hurt you."

I expected Marv to holler anytime, ask what the hold up was. I looked toward the door, and they were standing there, the Putzier Brothers, both of them, watching us. Baldy was gritting his teeth and looking at the horse, nodding his head quickly and barely, almost like a shake, but a nod. Marv was looking at Officer's Citation's body. He gave Officer's Citation a thorough once over, and finally a quick glance at his eye, to see the things he could see when he looked them in the eye.

"Better get him cleaned up, Bass," Marv said.

Baldy slapped the top chain, just like out at the rail. "Good," he said, with a final nod.

I took Officer's Citation's halter out of the feed tub, opened it, held it in front of him, and he put his nose in it, held his head down while I buckled the latch. I snapped the cotton lead rope to the halter, and I led him to the tie ring and slipped the rope through from the top. I didn't tie it. If he pulled back, I wanted him to keep going, not tied by the head and raising hell.

I brushed his mane and tail with the card, a flat piece of plastic, con-caved a little, with plastic knobs on it, sort of a hairbrush. I tried not to make contact with the hide on his neck, not wanting to cause tenderness or irritation. He was dirty and dusty, the dirt coming to the surface during the rubdown, but an easy going over with the cotton wipe, and he looked as presentable as it was going to get this morning.

He was still a damn good looking horse in peak physical condition. Tonight was all going to depend on the fuel still in the tank. There was a lot of exhausted fuel clinging to the dirty, damp cotton cloth.

I put him on the walker, and he walked, but he still strutted. He had nothing to be humble about, and he still knew it.

Other than the horse, the groom had very little to strut about.

I stripped the old straw out of the stall, three full wheelbarrow loads. I would go down the shedrow, get a run at the ramp, up the ramp, tip, dump, and pull the wheelbarrow right side up and back out. I had to work fast, and not screw around if shitcarts were out, about, and waiting. I had a little more bounce in my step, more than I had earlier in the morning. I could see a ray of hope, and I really didn't mind eggs over easy.

I finished, pulled the water bucket, cleaned it out, and left it by the wash rack.

"Should I shampoo him?"

"Nah," Baldy said. "Dust don't add that much weight."

"How 'bout dried sweat?" I asked.

"That'll fuck you up, for damn sure," he said. "Go see if you can find Gookstetter."

"He'll be here at ten," Marv said. "Chingachgook is pretty steady. Gotta be, last Mohican on earth."

I didn't know what he was talking about, other than the farrier, John Gookstetter, was coming over at ten.

"I gotta do some work for Rizzutto today," I said.

"I'll get 'im, Bass," Marv said.

Marv telling me he can hold the horse for the farrier. Marv

174

was a good farrier too, as good as any I've seen. No doubt he could hold one.

"Bring us about a dozen oats and a couple of bags of Omolene, don't you think?" Baldy said to me.

"707," I said.

"707," he said, "twenty-five pounder, though. I don't want to be tripping over that big bastard. Bring me a bill."

"Sure."

I put my horse away and headed for the warehouse. Bill was there, and we began loading the Nissan.

"Whaddya think tonight?" Bill said.

"Probably not," I said, wincing as I tossed a sack of oats on the truck.

"Stepping up?" he asked. "Didn't come up that tough, did it?"

"Yeah," I said. "We had a bad night." I lifted the cardboard container of 707, shaped like an oversized coffee can, twenty-five pounds, and gently slid it onto the bed of the truck.

"What'd you do to your back?"

"Uh, we had kind of a bad night," I said.

"Let me see," he said, lifting my tee shirt in the back.

"Whoa," Bill said. "You go to a doctor?"

This guy and his doctors.

I was sitting on the seed of an idea, and it started to sprout then and there. I heaved another sack of oats on the truck, went to the stack of sweet feed, and said, "No, I'm alright."

I gingerly maneuvered a bag of sweet feed on to the truck, maybe a little more gingerly than necessary, and started for another.

Bill asked, "Any blood when you pee?" Bingo.

I eased the bag of sweet feed on the truck, completing Baldy's order. "Little bit," I lied.

175

"You need to go see a doctor," Bill said.

"I won't argue with you," I said, as I hooked a thumb toward the grain bags on the truck. "You mind if I drop this off at the barn first?"

I was convinced that I had bluffed him into a day off. The truth was, it was a nasty bruise, and a day off would do me good. The thing is, being raised by a cowboy, it never occurred to me I would be allowed to take a sick day when I could stand on my feet. Not only that, I was going to spend the night of that sick day at the races. I didn't believe I was in heaven, for some reason.

So I stayed around the barn most of the day, after dropping the grain and returning the truck. I never went to the doctor, and my kidneys miraculously stayed free of blood.

I stood in front of Officer's Citation's stall, leaned against the door frame, full of Motrin and actually feeling alright if I kept it stretched. We read the form together then, my horse and I. My calm horse was back, but it had to have taken a lot out of him. The hours passed slowly, but it wasn't so bad the rest of the day, and it began to feel like maybe we had a chance.

Finally, we were cleaned up and bridled, on our way to the receiving barn for our third race of the year. He was a little too easy to handle in the paddock, but when Marv legged the rider up, Officer's Citation pricked his ears forward and looked like he wanted to be a racehorse. I delivered him to Bux and headed for the snake pit.

He was acting fine, but I knew what I knew, and only bet five dollars across the board, and I probably bet a two dollar exacta box on something, spending nineteen dollars on the bet and not expecting much. I only had one drink, and I didn't hurry through it.

The snake pit could be pretty fun, now that I was friends with, or at least acquainted with, most of the people who hung out in front of the window overlooking the paddock. You could hear the Racing Secretary announcing, and Keith Davis doing the color commentary. "That prick's gonna fold," Keith would announce, his eyes glued to the tv, watching the horse on the front end. He was usually correct in his colorful predictions.

I walked out to the bench where Baldy was, and we watched the race there with Marv and Deke, Baldy and I at the bench, them at the rail. Not many butterflies tonight, but a few.

The horses jogged to the gate, loaded quickly, and were on the way. Officer's Citation was away well, and Vince kept him on the outside. He gradually fell back and ran along about seventh place, maybe ten lengths off the lead, and began to move forward at the three-eighths pole. He was moving well at the quarter pole, but by the time they hit the three-sixteenth pole, Vince was standing up and pulling back, blocked, and they had no chance after that. Officer's Citation continued running and ended up fifth, beaten only three lengths.

I picked Officer's Citation up at the finish line and he was tired, but not blowing very hard. Marv and Deke walked with me as we went across the infield, through the gap and back to the barn. I washed him, watered and cooled him out, broke open a bale of straw and shook it out. Deke had prepared the feed; we filled the water bucket, and put our horse away.

"Still got our conditions," Marv said, as we headed for the gate.

I walked through the cafe and got a coke for the drive home. I glanced at the menu board on the way out the door. Open menu tomorrow, no conditions, no restrictions, and no weight pull. Things could be worse.

177

Wheeling Back

Officer's Citations barn was the along the outside rail at the top of the picture. The pathway leading from the tote board on the right third of the infield is directly across the backstretch from his barn. In the left third of the photo, you can see the path from the paddock to the gap, used by the horses after the race.

There were a lot of things to do, decisions to analyze and make, and I got an important one out of the way first. I went with the ham and cheese omelet, wheat toast and hashbrowns. I never get tired of ham and cheese, and while it is never the first choice, it is almost always second.

This writing technique is called foreshadowing.

So, at this point, we haven't run second yet this year, and we've only been in the nightcap once. Six of our next seven races would be in the nightcap, and we would run second four times. All of them were disappointing, but, as I soon found out, second was a hell of a lot better than seventh. I just didn't know it yet. Officer's Citation taught me to be disappointed with second, and it was something I gradually had to unlearn. I'm not sure if I ever got there.

Back at the barn, we were good to go. While the tantrum Officer's Citation threw moving into the new stall took something out of him, he still had his big heart and ran a credible race in spite of all of it, and he would have been close if not for being shut off at the three-sixteenth pole.

The fifth-place finish added fifty-five dollars to his bankroll, bringing his earnings up to $935 for the year. He had paid his purchase price off with the win. It does give an indication, however, of how difficult it is to turn a profit in this game. A winter's worth of feed and the spring track and training expenses were still on the negative side of the ledger.

"You can make a small fortune in horse racing, Bass," Baldy said, "but you have to start with a large one." Wisdom from the bench.

The race didn't take much more out of Officer's Citation. He was cold and calm the next morning, and Marv and Baldy saw a chance to stretch him out a little. We entered in a race for $3200 claiming, never won three, going a mile and a sixteenth, a quarter mile further than his previous race. The race was scheduled for next Friday, August seventh. We were wheeling back six days after his previous race.

If we ran on Lasix, we couldn't do this, as a Lasix horse will still be losing water and weight for a few days after the race.

A few years later, Marv was in the hospital, and they were giving him Lasix. The nurse asked him how he was doing. "This damned Lasix," he said. "I wish we'd hurry up and enter."

We named Vince Ward to ride him back, taking the five-pound weight allowance. Baldy wasn't that happy with the last ride, but the win had given Vince the right to a couple more chances.

You would think with wheeling him back this quickly, there would be something to do at the barn. He had no leg issues, no heat or swelling, no soreness either, so it wasn't really even necessary to do his legs up with mud. We only did it once that week, the day after the race.

His new shoes were good, so I went back to the Hooflex, every other day. Other than that, we walked him up to the race, never taking him to the track that week. To keep him from destroying the stall, I would take him out for a tour of the barnyard and let him eat grass every time I got a chance.

Other than that, hurry up and wait. Two days after the race, four days before the next, and we were back to stress testing snaps. The brass was still stretching, but the zinc was holding. Cole 1, Officer's Citation 27, but at least I was on the board.

With the exception of one temporary chain link tattoo on my back, it was like the circus last week never happened. He didn't seem to mind his new stall much, after the initial meltdown. I think he simply exhausted himself and surrendered.

Friday arrived just after midnight Thursday, right on schedule. So far, so good. There was no point in getting to the track early, but my eyes usually popped open on race days around five in the morning. I may have mentioned, I'm not really a morning person, but you would be amazed at how a racehorse in the barn changes your attitude when the alarm goes off. Getting paid to hang around the racetrack is a good life.

I drove down before six in the morning on my motorcycle,

a little 650 Yamaha Special road bike. As I drove past the grandstand toward Haven street, on the north end of the track, on the opposite side of the fence from the clubhouse turn just past the finish line, I noticed a bum running toward me and waving, running to catch me. Against every one of my better instincts, I stopped and waited.

My instincts were correct. It was Keith Davis.

"Hey, Clay," he said, climbing on behind me. "Thanks for stopping."

"I knew it was you, I'da kept going."

"Ya fucked up," he said. "How fast does this thing go?"

I was in a stretch where I had received three tickets in about four weeks. I pulled the same judge in traffic court for the first and the third. He was a very lenient and reasonable judge the first time, and kind of a prick a couple of weeks later, for some reason.

"Have I seen you before?" his honor said.

I didn't answer, as I assumed I had that right.

"Speak up," he said.

"I dunno," was my unenthusiastic and untrue response.

I do know that I didn't want to see his honor ever again. I didn't get a reduction on the ticket.

"It doesn't go very fast anymore," I said to Keith.

"Faster than that little brown prick, I hope," he said, insulting my horse.

I revved the engine and dumped the clutch, but he held on.

Picking Keith up in the mornings became sort of a tradition. He started leaving a little earlier so he didn't have to run, and so I started leaving earlier so he would have to run. Training him up. You could have some fun with Keith.

I once told Keith about getting bucked off a Thoroughbred,

and his only question was, "Did you hold on to the reins?"

"Yes," I said.

"Good."

The truth is, the reins were the only thing I had left to hold on to. The rest of the equipment was still attached to a filly who was about five feet below me and getting further away by the second.

Keith and I buzzed around the clubhouse turn and into the backstretch, and parked taking advantage of the favorable spot afforded to motorcycles, right outside the gate.

We walked through the gate together, and Keith peeled off to go to his barn, down in the hole by the clubhouse turn. I headed toward the gap. I would return to the cafe for coffee and breakfast after feeding. Keith didn't drink coffee in the morning, maybe ever. But he would accept a beer at six in the morning if you were to offer.

I went over Officer's Citation pretty well, legs, feet, back, all systems go. I tossed a can of oats in the feed tub and went to the rail, and then the cafe. Baldy showed up, we shuffle staggered to the barn, and I stripped Officer's Citation's stall and pulled the water bucket, finishing by nine. I'm not going to try to convince you I remembered specifics this many years later, but the routine was the routine.

This journal is based on a true story, with no more lies in it than you would normally find on the backstretch.

That being said, some of the emotions and specifics, I can recall vividly.

I would have worked from ten to about five, and with four hours before I had to do anything at all, it was probably home for a shower after happy hour at the Stockyards. I never minded missing the early races, so I would guess I arrived around six thirty, about the time they were getting ready to run the second race. I bought a program for the night's races, checked on my horse, and at the guinea stand or the cafe watched the days races on the closed-circuit monitors. You could bet at the guinea stand, but not the cafe.

There is a certain smell around the backstretch at that time of night, near the guinea stand, when the races are running. The sun is setting, and the smell of the hot plywood, mixed with the years of dust inside, combined with cigarette smoke in the fresh air, maybe a whiff of bark from the flowerbeds, and it just sort of takes me back. The smell of cigarette smoke wafting past in the fresh air is the one smell that really takes me there. Cigar smoke, too. You can smell the grass and the vegetation, and get a close-up view of what happens after the post parade, and before the starting gate.

The horses come to the paddock before the race, are saddled, exit and turn right onto the track, coming out of the paddock at about the eighth pole. They are then picked up by a pony, to escort them to the starting gate. The pony is contracted privately, not assigned. Marv's heart problems were probably caused by the pony not showing up for the race throughout the years. He did love a good closer, though, so the heart problems weren't all caused by unreliable ponies.

Assuming they are all here, the ponies are more or less in line, one to ten, front to back, the first one being at the gap coming out of the paddock. If it is an opening for horses to go onto the track, it is called a gap. Unless it is one of the chutes on the end of the track, then it's just the chute.

As the riders are legged up in order, one through however many are in the race, the groom leads the Thoroughbred onto the track, and since the correct side to pony a horse is from the left and to the right, I went straight to the horse. The pony boy or girl would hand me a thin, about eighth inch thick and three-quarter inch wide leather strap three or four feet long. I would run this through the ring that connects the bit to the headstall, and double it back and hand it to the pony boy or girl.

It sort of becomes like a choreographed thing at that point. The bugler plays the call to post as the number one groom hands his horse off and pushes his way out from between the pony and the racer, wary of being kicked by either, but more likely watching the Thoroughbred closer. Once he is clear of the hind end of his horse, he can either get clear out on the track past the ponies, or he can get back across the rail past the Thoroughbreds, usually opting for the rail and taking a quick step or two to avoid the number two horse who has just been handed off. If you go to the track side of the horses, you run the risk of being in the way as they gallop back wrong way of the track after the post parade. It is better to run the Thoroughbred side of the gauntlet and get all the way out of the way.

The groom has to fend for his or her self during this exchange, as the pony riders and jockeys have plenty to do themselves at this point. It is not hurried, but there is a rhythm to it. Handoff, get out from between, quick, but easy so as not to spook any horses with quick, unexpected movement. Cross the path of the number two thoroughbred and go over the rail, and watch out you don't get kicked as the two horse goes by. Keep those hot-blooded Thoroughbreds moving is the rule of thumb before races.

If they are right where you want them, they are on the verge of blowing their top, and the fuse burns way faster when they are standing still. Like in the starting gate.

The process repeats ten times, the horses are on the track

as the echo from the call to post fades, and the post parade is underway. They file past the stands, the horses on the grandstand side so the gamblers and race fans can get a look, the announcer calling out the number, name of the horse, the owner, the trainer, and the jockey, and moves to number two. The camera stays with the announcer as long as he can, but if the announcer is slow, he will have to call the names out as they are making the u-turn around the outrider just past the finish line. The one horse is now turned and jogging wrong way of track, and the ten is still on the paddock end, parading past the grandstand.

The other outrider will be near the far turn, adjacent to the paddock, and as the one horse and pony approach, he will start to jog, and eventually gallop to a spot on the backstretch where it receives the clubhouse turn, all the way around to the half-mile chute. The racehorses will be led by their ponies, usually at a slow gallop, until they form a rough circle, not really in order, in the vicinity of the guinea stand.

Some of the horses will gallop to the clubhouse turn if the jockey feels like the horse isn't quite right, or if he needs a longer warm up. It can drive you nuts watching a jockey leave your race in the warm-up. You have to trust them, the crooked little sonsabitches, as Marv would say.

At two minutes to post, the starter will yell, or radio, depending, "Bring 'em up!" and the horses will re-shuffle into numerical order as they walk to the starting gate. "Hurry up!" will bring them to a jog, but they usually are allowed to walk. The first race is the only one that ever starts on time, so the post times are usually a half hour late, at least, by the time you get to the nightcap.

Bad gate horses are kept on a list by the starter, either on paper or the ticker tape that most racetrackers have in their heads, and loaded either first or last, depending. There is nothing worse than watching a horse throw a two-minute tantrum while yours is standing quietly in the gate. Quietly in the gate for two minutes is not something you hear, or see, often at the track.

The fuse is a lot shorter on those amped up sprinting Quarter Horses. Nitroglycerin is more stable than a two-year-old Quarter Horse at the starting gate, and slightly less explosive. You never knew with any given Thoroughbred, either. The fuses were always burning.

The starting gate is it's own choreographed process, sometimes two horses are loaded at a time, starting with one and six, or one at a time in numerical order. The veterans usually just walk right in. Sprinters are a little worse at the gate than routers, but ninety-five percent of the horses will walk in and stand. The fuse burns faster the minute the gate closes behind them.

An assistant starter leads the horse in, usually two starters on either side of the horse also. The good gate crews can have the gate loaded and ready in less than half a minute if all goes well. Once inside the gate, the assistant starter beside the horse's head climbs up on a narrow platform beside the horse, his feet level with the bottom of the horse's belly. He has the horse held lightly and firmly by the headstall and is responsible for having the horse's head straight at the break. The only warning the break is coming is when the assistant starter says "All in."

Horrific things can happen at the starting gate, and you always hold your breath a little until they spring the latch. If it has a heartbeat and is on a racetrack, there are dozens of ways for it to sustain an injury on race day.

The stands, however, are pretty much safe from everything

but heart attacks induced by late running closers falling in on a collapsing speed horse. It can give you a thrill.

"They're all in line," spits the PA. Bang, bang, bang, a horse begins to unravel in the gate, maybe yours, maybe the one next to him, maybe not. A split second of silence, a muted slam as the starter presses the button and ten gates simultaneously open, a bell rings, sounds just like the bell telling you class is about to start. If you watch from the side of the gate, you see ten horses simultaneously drop about four inches as they leap into stride from a standing start.

"There they go!"

And for a minute and change, there is hope that you might pay the rent tonight. The show bettor laments the loss of his two dollars, the bridge jumper looks for a tout, the degenerate on the rail only missed by one and chews his cigar, focused on the racing form.

I guess I like the grandstand side too.

Time to get my horse ready. He's got his head out of the stall as I turn the corner, always a good sign. Taking an interest. He gives me a knicker, and I walk over and scratch him on both sides of his neck.

"You ready, big hoss?" I asked. I didn't like to call him little on race days.

He nodded, rubbing his forehead on my chest.

One thing at a time, cotton lead rope, hoof pick, Hooflex.

From the ground up, feet first. Start at the left front, back, under his belly, pick the dirt out, hold the foot up, blow the dust out, apply a very thin first coat, and it dries in about ten seconds. Very thin, and add a drop of denatured alcohol to the brush to help speed the dry time. Just a drop. If you smear it on, it will stay wet for ten minutes.

So I did learn something useful painting houses, after all.

Two or three thin coats on the bottom of the hoof, wait until it dries. I reach behind and grasp the leg, not letting it hit the ground as I crouch under his shoulder. His hoof is resting on my knee as I support his leg and brush off the dust. I then brush a thicker coat on the exterior of the hoof and set it down gently, letting it dry while he stands on it and I move to the left hind.

The trick is to use a light hand, don't force his legs, a little pressure the only force you want to exert. Go easy, take your time, keep him calm, be efficient. Talk to him a little, it will be good for both of you. It will mitigate your chances of getting kicked.

The hind legs, you prop on the inside of your knee when you bring it back, never straight out. Up and then back. Don't pin it between your legs. If he pulls his leg back, you step back quick with your inside leg, ahead of his hind leg if you can get there soon enough. Do not have your leg planted when he kicks, it hurts like hell. Officer's Citation wasn't a kicker, though, the worst he would do is snatch his foot from you if you screwed around too long.

Same process on the other side, front to back. Put the Hooflex away, reach for the hand cleaner and try to get that crap off my hands. Or just let it dry, it will peel off soon enough. Shellac is a self-priming product, however, so it takes a while.

Some people aren't superstitious on the backstretch, in fact, most of them aren't. It would shock you if I told you how many black cats I have seen in the barn area. Put a four leaf clover on your silks, and bring a black cat to the barn. Just asking for trouble. I had a pretty good feeling about the race, so I was alert, of course. I didn't see the need for any special rituals, though.

About 9:45, the PA barked, "Attention horsemen, bring your

horses to the receiving barn for the tenth race. Horses to the receiving barn for the tenth."

Marv said, "Wait."

Officer's Citation pricked his ears, I stood quietly. He was dry as a bone. Damp spots were appearing at my flanks.

Off in the distance from down in the hole, you can hear the clippety-clop of aluminum shoes on pavement, one coming up the lane nearest the track, one of them coming up the lane one shedrow east. Two men and a horse, one groom and one trainer emerge out of the darkness in between the lamps, the trainer nods to Marv.

"How you doing, Marv," says Darrell Butterfield, leading a recent graduate of his never won two condition race. Darrell taps his horse on the shoulder, points to mine, and says, "That's the one you gotta watch out for, right there."

It's respect, and it feels good.

I lead Officer's Citation out of his stall, all the way into the shedrow before turning right, Deke walking beside me as I fall in behind Darrell. "Ima try an' keep him right there," Darrell says to Marv, as we head to the receiving barn.

It isn't long before we arrive at the receiving barn, and Deke has the headstall number on before we make it to the stall. I make one circuit and turn into the stall, head him in and he won't stand still. I head out, make one more circuit of the small paddock in the receiving barn, and try again, this time heading out. He stands still, surveying the competition, his ears pricked forward, not looking too impressed or acting nervous at all.

"To your stalls please." We hear the cheers coming from the grandstand as they charge to the wire in the ninth.

"Attention horsemen, bring your horses to the paddock for the tenth race. Horses to the paddock for the tenth." We step out of the stall at once, simultaneously with the rest of the horses, turn left and we are in line, headed for the paddock. I walk a little to the side of the horse in front, about ten feet behind. I want the horse to know where I am, whether the groom does or not.

It's peaceful, still around seventy degrees as we walk over, cooling down finally, perfect weather to race. Not much activity here except for the horses going to the paddock, the horses not in tonight having been fed four hours ago. Some of them ignore us as we walk past, others stand with their ears pricked, a nervous horse quivers, and a sour old gelding charges the chains, his ears pinned back.

But we move on, not much talking, everyone thinking about the job ahead, about the race. Marv draws a line in the air with his index finger pointed toward the ground, from Officer's Citation to the stall, meaning don't take a circuit, come straight to the stall.

"In or out, Bass?" Marv asking my opinion on how we saddle, head in or out.

"Out," I say, "He likes to take a look."

"Head out," he says, pointing and swooping that index finger, a signal code Deke and I learned long ago, Marv giving me a quick nod, just one.

I lead Officer's Citation into the stall, slip the rein over his head as we turn, and bring him to a stop. I slide the rein forward on his neck so it doesn't interfere with the saddling, and work the bit back and forth as much as it is possible with a nine hundred pound athlete leaning against me. Quickly and efficiently, the horse is saddled and ready almost before he comes to a stop. Marv swoops his finger toward the paddock, choreographing the ballet in stall nine of the saddling paddock.

"Give him a turn, Bass."

We're back to walking, and we're dealing with a tougher horse than we were five minutes ago. He's not turning a hair, but coming up on his toes, on the muscle. Perfect, in a perfect state of mind, on a perfect night in early August.

"Riders!"

One more circuit while the riders are given instructions to ignore.

"Put your horses in, please!" Lightfoot barks. He waits a moment, surveying the scene, "Come on now, one!" He pauses a moment, "Two! Three! Four, there ya go, Five!" Finally, I hear nine, and I'm not listening anymore, I'm headed for the gap onto the track. The call to post is being bugled, the cigar smoke drifts, the strap is looped and handed off. Officer's Citation is on the track, and I'm down the stairs, twelve steps on the tarmac and up the ramp, into the snake pit, where Deke has a shot of tequila and a beer waiting for me.

"Ta kill ya!" he says, and we shoot the shot, hammer the beer and head to the window. Twenty across the board, two dollar exacta nine with all, and back to the bar. We do another shot and split a beer, two gulps apiece and it's gone. Then out to the bench, standing on it while Baldy sits below, Marv and Deke at the rail.

The routine was the routine, and it was followed.

They're loading, they're in, they're off, and we settle in mid-pack, about ten off the pace, running easy. Everything is good for the first circuit, then Officer's Citation moves at the three-eighths pole, and Baldy says, "Goddamnit, too soon."

But he's moving forward, really rolling at the quarter pole and he's stretching out, a length and a half clear at the eighth pole, but there's one running late, that horse dropping down from four thousand claiming, and getting it done. He goes by Officer's Citation at the sixteenth, running past a tired horse who moved just a little too soon, and we run second, beaten three lengths, a neck in front of the third-place horse.

He was thirteen to one, and I did a little better than break even on the place and show money. He pulled up gradually, nearly all the way to the quarter pole, the rider not wanting to hear about being told to wait until they hit the quarter pole. But they gallop back, the rider salutes the stewards with his whip, indicating that he had a good trip and was not interfered with. He then unsaddles the horse with the valet, makes a few excuses for Marv as he does so, and we are back in motion and headed for the test barn again.

I look around for the young lady with the test barn tag, and she can't find us, we are unsaddled so quickly. I catch her eye and point to the test barn, say "It's this way," smiling, joking with her, already on the way to the bark pathway across the infield.

She might have smiled, but it sure looked like a dirty look from where I was. I had pretty good eyes back then. She ran, caught up to us, snapped the test tag on his bridle, and we walked over in silence, her looking straight ahead, me leaning against my horse, half walking, half jogging. He's blowing a little and snorting as I rub and pat his neck.

Marv, walking beside, said, "Looks like he come back okay."

"Yeah, I think so,"

"We'll have the stall ready for you," he said, peeling to the right as my horse and I turned left and headed for the test barn, second time in the last three tries.

We head to the test barn, shampoo, cool the horse out, water him out and put him in the stall. I don't go in, knowing it will be a while, and it seemed a little chilly in there anyway, what with the test barn official not having much of a sense of humor. I read the form for a few minutes and went to the stall. I usually tried to witness the entire chain of custody of the urine sample as much as they did in the test barn since I had to sign for the sample.

We waited, and waited some more, and I topped off his water bucket. It wasn't very long before we were alone in a totally silent test barn, just the three of us. The horse was tired, and I was a little disappointed but feeling pretty good. The test barn official, who was about twenty-one years old, didn't seem all that happy to be working late on Friday night.

About one o'clock, he stretched out and squirted a little, but she was good at her job and got the sample.

"I sure love that horse," she said. "He's such a cutie."

"What's your name?" I asked.

"Sign here," she said, "I gotta lock up."

"Okay." I signed.

She rubbed Officer's Citation on the forehead.

"See you next time," she said as I led a little brown Thorough-bred back to the barn.

Spun

The John Deere model 6602 hillside combine harvesting wheat in the Palouse country

Officer's Citation was subdued the next morning, having been asked to give it all and giving it. An older rider named Ron Chappell came by the barn, on the downhill side of a good career. He was only riding five percent winners, and not getting

194

many mounts, but anyone on the backstretch who knew would tell you he was a hell of a rider in his day.

"Marv," he said, "I'm not going to undercut the kid, but if you want to make a change, I think I could help that horse."

"Well, Chappell," Marv said, "As we stretch him out, he's just gonna have to run the fractions, twenty-three and change for the quarter or thereabouts, and just kind of keep him off the pace, and I think he'll be ok."

"He's live gear," said Chappell. "I'd like the shot you make the change."

"Whose got your book?" asked Marv.

"Hobbs," said Chappell.

Bill Hobbs was another friend, more trainer than agent, and knew Marv and Baldy from way back. We were making a change.

"Don't fall in love with a God damned jockey," Baldy said and lived by it.

Vince had three chances, got one win, one second, and one fourth on Officer's Citation, but Marv and Baldy thought he cost them the last race by moving too soon. They forgave the fifth place for reasons already detailed but weren't happy about him running into a blind switch; an opening, but not a hole. Nothing personal, just business.

It helped that Chappell could still give you a masterful ride once in a while. A lot of agents were skulking around, but Baldy gave Hobbs a call, and he gave us first call on Chappell.

I may have mentioned that agents were somewhat unscrupulous about spinning a trainer, but Hobbs was a good friend, so no worries there.

That sonofabitch Hobbs spun us.

Chappell was named on a horse named Bear Dog, simply

because Bear Dog came from a stable four times the size of our one-horse operation. Bear Dog would save a jock mount for you, and hit the board occasionally, but he wanted no part of the Little Provolone.

Officer's Citation ended up beating Bear Dog by a wide margin, with Vince riding Officer's Citation once again. Normally, if you don't name rider at the draw, you don't get the weight allowance on the bug. But Vince's agent, a man whose name I didn't know because Baldy always just called him double oh seven, named Vince on after Hobbs did his agent thing, so we got the weight pull, and Hobbs got fired by Chappell.

Chappell never got to ride Officer's Citation, but we did cycle through some riders in the last few races.

Officer's Citation ended up with fifteen days between races, and I ended up at the farm for harvest. I enjoyed the money but was getting tired of the psychology being directed toward me due to the pay raise.

One hundred divided by sixteen hours a day was six dollars and twenty-five cents an hour, straight time. Everyone on the farm was driving a car or truck less than two years old, they had a ski boat, two snow mobiles and a whole bunch of other toys that led me to believe that it was going to take more than six twenty-five to break the bank. They spent more on beer than I could afford on rent. And I didn't begrudge them any of it, in fact I benefited from some of it due to the adopted son status I had briefly attained within the family.

I learned something way more valuable, though. I learned that loyalty was a one-way street when it came to employers and employees. I made this observation to Marv Saturday morning as we drank coffee and read the Wall Street, his name for the Daily Racing Form.

"I'll tell you what," said Marv, "A guy gives you the raise but acts like that, you owe him a hundred bucks worth of effort a day, and that's all you owe him." He continued, "He's been good to you, so think about it before you do anything can't be undone."

Good advice. I threw a for what it's worth on the table that told him where my mind was.

"It ain't like I want to be on the farm, anyway," I said. "It isn't personal, but I just don't understand somebody doesn't want to see what's over the next hill."

"Couldn't wait to leave the farm behind, myself, Bass," he said. "I reckon it's in your pedigree."

It seemed like I had permission to get off the farm, but Marv had one more golden nugget of advice.

"You go down there, keep your mouth shut, and work like you do," he said. "Collect your check, shake the man's hand whether he looks you in the eye or not, and let the chips fall." He paused. "You made your deal, you stick to it. He pays you off, then it's all up to you after that."

It was damned good advice. The relationship was broken, but there was no need to throw rocks as I walked away. It was the best way to handle the situation.

I learned a lot on the farm, but I would never learn to love it. It wasn't a bad life, it just wasn't for me. I saw Los Angeles when I was seventeen, and that sealed the deal on the farm.

Baldy told me to tell the guy to get fucked.

There were quite a few reasons he was the favorite uncle, even if I didn't always take his advice.

"Why don't you hustle some book?" he said.

"Cha," I said.

"I'm serious."

"No chance," I said. "I don't like talking to people, and I don't know how. I have to tell the truth just to keep my story straight. I don't want any part of being an agent."

Just then Russ Janish walked in and sat down. Baldy said, "On the other hand," flipping the good bad hand toward Russ, "you see how bad it can all go."

"What the hell are you into now?" Russ said to Baldy as I laughed.

"Bass wants to be an agent," said Baldy.

"He's too honest for that," said Russ, " I ask him the other day about the horse, and I'm pretty sure he told me the truth."

Russ didn't know it, but he had just buried me.

"He might need to learn to keep his mouth shut," said Marv.

Point taken, and not the first time I'd heard it.

Baldy arched an eyebrow at me, Russ looked back and forth between the brothers.

I drank my coffee and lost myself in the form.
*****

"You gonna tout a guy?" Bill asked, later that day.

"No, hell no," I said.

Bill giggled. "Learning, aren't you?"

I raised an eyebrow, glanced at him, kept loading grain. "Maybe."

"He oughta be tough."

"I don't know nuthin'."

Bill giggled.
*****

Officer's Citation had added another three hundred thirty dollars to his earnings, now at twelve hundred sixty-five dollars for the year, about three hundred ten dollars a month on average. It may have paid for the hay, but that was about it.

Out of those earnings, we had a hundred ninety-three in jock's fees, forty for the pony. It was not a money-making proposition at the bottom of the claiming ladder. It was still just as much fun to win races, though.

We had a little different routine now that we were stretching Officer's Citation out to longer races. During the week, it was the same, as far as I knew. We'll get to that in a day or two. Turns out, I had some business to take care of in the Palouse.

I was on the farm, and harvest in the Palouse was in full swing. I harvested peas and lentils, the boss and I operating the two older combines, John Deere 6602 model, the 02 designating hillside. The problem was, now that I was earning a good wage, I couldn't do anything right.

In reality, my machine was running fine; two weeks in and no breakdowns. The boss, however, was having some problems and he was still pissed off at me for having the audacity to ask for a raise, still trying to school me. If I was working for less money, he'd have been pretty happy with me.

It was a lesson I had no intention to take with me when I left the farm. I wasn't taking anything when I left the farm, as far as I knew. If he wasn't going to be cutting before me in the morning due to mechanical problems, he would take the trap wagon and go to the shop to do his repairs. I would be ready to go, but no trap wagon, no fuel.

The first time it happened, I cut a couple of loads of the bulk tank in the combine, about half a truckload. Dangerously low on fuel, I headed back to the flat to wait for the trap wagon, and for the boss to show back up to the field. He had returned to the field and was pulling away from the trapwagon in his combine when I reached the flat. He announced on the radio that he was cutting, and he didn't know what I was doing.

So the next time he took off with the trap wagon, I stayed in the flat and read the racing form until he got back.

If you can't win at work, you might as well give yourself a chance to win at the track.

The Palouse country is made up of rolling hills, the most fertile dryland wheat producing region in the nation. It isn't made up of anything other than rolling hills. We called the valleys draws, not valleys. Most of the fields had a five or ten acre flat, an area by the road that was, of course, flat. These flats were usually divided by gravel roads, separating the fields. Otherwise, one hill began where the last one ended.

There was a trick to harvesting and cultivating these hills, you had to go with the contour, and if you didn't 'lay it off' correctly on the backland, or backlash, I have heard it both ways, you could end up in trouble on the corners as they migrated up the hillside with each swath of the combine.

The backland was where the dirt would form a ridge where you plowed going one way in the flat, and the other on the hillside. It was hard for an inexperienced eye to see, and I realized that if it wasn't shaped like a Thoroughbred, I wasn't very interested in learning about it. Even before the Thoroughbreds came along I knew I wasn't destined to be a farmer.

Baldy used to say, "Once a farmer, always a farmer," everytime I went back to the Palouse. We both knew he was wrong about that one.

It was usually pretty uneventful, but about once every five or ten years, someone would roll a combine, or tip one over sliding off a hill, and it usually resulted in death. It wasn't unusual for someone to lose an arm or leg to the various mechanical equipment necessary for commercial farming and grain storage.

You had to pay attention. It was hours of boredom surrounding a few moments of high anxiety.

Some of the hills were very steep, long, and covered with slick wheat straw. Peas and lentils were easier to harvest for one reason only, your tires were always on dirt. As I said, I learned a lot on the farm, but all I ever wanted from the Palouse country was out of it, forever.

That years experience was not doing anything to keep me on the farm.

I shut the machine down next to the trap wagon on Friday night, and we rode back to the shop in silence. I hopped out of the truck before it stopped rolling, and headed for the Yamaha.

"Hey, we need you tomorrow," he said.

"I got a horse in tomorrow, fuckhead," I said, "I'll either be back Monday, or you can fire me now."

I was tired of his shit, and decided I had had enough of the farm to last me a lifetime.

"What would your Dad say about that?" he hollered after me, knowing where I got the work ethic I had.

He wasn't sure where I got the temper, but he had seen it before. This was a very dysfunctional family business, and it was not a huge offense to call someone a derogatory name in the heat of the moment. I'd been here five years, and I could have picked it up from him. I turned on my heal and walked back over to him.

"I'll tell you what he said about that," I said. "He said I made the deal I made, and owed you a day's work for a day's pay, to shake your hand when it was all said and done, and whether you looked me in the eye or not, be a man about it."

"Oh, he did?"

"Yeah," I said. "He did. But my uncle told me to tell you to get fucked, and I'm starting to think I took the wrong advice."

I had a full-time job waiting at the track, and I was trying to get fired.

The boss wasn't used to anything but total subservience, so this was unusual for him. It wasn't that easy to find a combine operator in the middle of harvest, however. Not impossible, but not that easy. And like any bully, he would back down if you called him on his BS. I had learned this in a previous altercation.

"You coming back Monday?"

"Am I? I'm trying to think of a reason why I would."

"I can think of a hundred reasons," he said.

I stepped over toward him, about eighteen inches between us. He was six two and tacked about two forty, and I was five nine, tacked about one seventy. I was pissed off and ready to try him, though, consequences be damned.

"How much bullshit comes with those one hundred reasons?" I asked, very quietly, looking him in the eye.

"None, kid," he said. "We don't have a problem."

"Have we had a problem?" I asked, "Cause if we haven't, then I ain't interested in your definition of no bullshit."

"We don't have a problem, Cole," he said. "It's always been good between us, I don't want it to change." He reached out, offering to shake hands. I extended mine, and we shook.

"I need you tomorrow," he said.

"I got a horse in tomorrow. You want me to choose, I will."

"We'll see you Monday, I guess," he said, with a little bit of an edge to his voice. We had crossed a bridge that wasn't going to be uncrossed.

I headed for Spokane, still pretty amped up. I ran into Deke at the Stockyards and had a better time than I expected. Hooker always treated me pretty well, and sometimes, so did everyone else.

Renovation Break

Looking out the window toward the west as the sun goes down on a lazy evening in the spring, I can see three Thoroughbreds. They are grazing and enjoying the last few sun rays of the day, their tails swatting at the flies who accompany the warm weather. The horses have eaten their grain, and are beginning to stir a little.

It is difficult to say what, but something is in the air, and maybe it is just an excuse to run delivered by a warm and gentle spring breeze. Whatever it is swoops into the center paddock of three, all identical and trimmed by hedges a deeper shade of green.

A slight puff on a tuft of dried grass is all it takes, the only excuse the majestic Thoroughbred needs to toss his head and begin to trot. His neighbors heed his call, and in unison the three powerful steeds trot to the end of the paddock near the road. They slowly make the turn and still in line they easily gallop, returning to the other end, two hundred feet, not quite a sixteenth of a mile. Long, powerful and easy strides bring them to the fence, where they pull up in a cloud of dust and flying tufts of dirt and grass.

But it is not the end of the session, nor even a respite. With a toss of that beautiful head, the near one is turning again, and running with a little more power this time. As one, still in unison, a little faster do they gallop to the other end, tails trailing behind, manes blowing in the breeze they have generated.

From near to far, they are colored bay, chestnut and gray, one old, one young, and one in his prime, leading them this time as they circle back. They slacken their gait as they come back from the far end this time, heads and tails in the air; they bounce to a stop, and paw, and snort.

When the young one, knowing only pedigree and instinct lays the gantlet down and sprints out to the lead, the others hear the bugle blow the call to post. The grass is pulled beneath their feet, clumps and clods raining down behind them as they lunge away from the start and toward the wire, the youngster showing some speed as he noses out the big horse this time.

Never count the old campaigner out, his joints and muscles loose by now. He bows his neck and shows the youngsters how. Beckoning triumphs past, the heart of the Thoroughbred, the most powerful muscle in that sculpted body, is pumping hot blood from the mighty genes of his ancestors through his veins. He instinctively feels the need to compete, and he leads them to the wire this time. They all throw their heads and snort and grunt. They kick, they buck, and they play.

Then as if it were post time, they all hear the bell at the same time and they thunder to the road for real, barely slackening speed as they round the turn for home. In a few giant, powerful strides, they go from full out to a sliding stop as they come to the fence.

The Thoroughbreds run back and forth along the fence a little, gradually easing into a trot. They slowly wind down and give that majestic head one last shake. They cool themselves out, swish a tail and don't think about tomorrow.

Nailed

I arrived early, sporting a decent hangover, tired from no sleep, and feeling pretty good due to the events that led to no sleep. I headed for the apartment in Spokane, grabbed a quick shower and a change of clothes. Then it was off to the track. I arrived at around seven, late for me these days, but still an hour early.

Officer's Citation had a can of whole oats, and I had biscuits and gravy at the cafe, superstition taking a backseat for a hangover breakfast tradition that never actually helped that much. I got a coffee and headed for the barn, taking a quick detour to the restroom in the barn area when the biscuits and gravy threatened to boomerang and made it just in time. I rinsed my mouth out with water and threw away the coffee, ran some water over my head and took a long drink out of the hose at the barn.

And I had a half day for Rizzuto today, a load of straw by myself on the agenda from a field near Medical Lake, about twenty miles away. I tried to convince myself that I felt better.

But before straw and after breakfast, Bux came over for the horse, and Baldy and I followed to the rail.

"Once around real easy," Baldy said to Bux.

We were taking Officer's Citation to the track the morning of the race with a pony, just trying to take the edge off a little bit. Officer's Citation played all the way around the track and kicked with his left hind leg until we heard a pop that sounded like a rifle shot, and then he settled down into a steady slow gallop, just barely faster than a jog.

"Popped his back," Baldy told me. "He oughta be alright for the race. We'll get the chip in a day or two, looks like he might be getting a little sore."

Chip being the chiropractor, Marv's abbreviation.

He was a little sore, I had noticed it when I wiped him down this morning, but he was feeling pretty good as he played on the walker while I stripped his stall. We were in the nightcap, so we pulled the water bucket around nine, right before Baldy went home, and I went to work.

I got the old Ford, a 1972 two ton box truck, an old moving van with a logo I couldn't quite make out showing through the thin white coat of paint applied over the top. They should have used a light gray automotive primer first, but nobody asked me.

I headed out, taking Haven street past the track, right on Sprague, left on Altamont, right on second, and onto Interstate ninety, twenty-two miles to Medical Lake, another three to the field. I arrived a little after ten.

I parked in between the stacks of straw and laid down in the seat to catch a couple of hours sleep. I couldn't fall asleep, but when I looked at my watch, it was approaching noon. I had dozed a couple of hours, but if anything, I felt worse.

I loaded the straw pretty fast, the sweat therapy actually helping quite a bit. The straw was light and clean, not very dusty at all. I drove back to Medical Lake, bought a cold six pack of coke, guzzled two of them immediately, ripped a huge belch, and felt ready to face the rest of the day. I didn't ever want two jobs ever again, but I had very few regrets about late nights in those days.

I fired up the truck, popped the two speed rear end into low, and headed into town the back way. I took Sunset highway down the hill, found my way to Sprague Avenue, jogged over to Trent Avenue on Napa, and turned right, about a half mile to the ugly yellow Quonset hut.

I backed the Ford into the warehouse, parked, locked up, hopped on the Yamaha, and headed for the apartment Deke and I shared. I crawled into bed at about three o'clock, setting the alarm for five thirty. I fell asleep immediately, and thirty seconds later, the alarm went off at five thirty.

Ugh. I closed my eyes. The alarm buzzed again, at five thirty-nine. Again at five forty-eight.

OK, race day, you haven't already forgotten the speech you made on the farm yesterday, have you?

It seemed like a long time ago. A quick shower rejuvenated me, though. I guzzled the last Coke and headed to the track.

I arrived around six fifteen, purchased a program in the cafe, and saw that we were picked to run third in the race, morning line odds of five to one. The days of cashing big tickets on Officer's Citation were over. This was a pattern that was to become familiar to me for one of Marv's horses, big odds on his first couple of races, nice odds on the third, and no odds after one or two more.

So I either had to find a way to include every horse with a chance in the trifecta or just light my money on fire. Or box him both ways in the exacta, and spend thirty-six dollars to collect on a nine dollar ticket. It appeared the bonfire was the best alternative, but no fires were allowed in the stable area, and no smoking in the shedrow.

It looked like a horse named Margo's Flag was going to be tough. We had raced against him a few times previously, finishing behind him twice, and ahead of him once. It looked like we might have a pace to run down, but there were two or three of us with a legitimate shot to win. This wasn't quite as easy as I thought it was going to be.

Maybe just not bet?

That was good for a chuckle to myself, and I headed to the barn.

I gave my horse a sip of water, and he went back to standing with his back legs in the hole that had appeared in the back of the stall recently. He was a little sore in the back.

Marv arrived, and said, "He doesn't have his head out." He walked over to the stall.

"Standing in a hole," I said.

"Go get a bucket of hot water," Marv said. "Just a little south of red ripping."

Which meant as hot as you can get it, a splash of cold. I went to the wash rack and got the water as Marv went to the white box in the tack room, trimmed in black, about two feet tall, eighteen inches deep and eighteen wide, hanging on the tack room wall. This is where we kept the mud, wraps, vitamins, and liniments, and Marv came back with a plastic pint bottle of bigeloil as I arrived with the water at the stall.

"Rinse that big sponge out, real clean," Marv said. "Get the light cooler."

I went to the tack room, located the light cotton cool out blanket, grabbed a new wash sponge from the shelf I bought before the last race but didn't have to use, Officer's Citation getting his planned bath from his admiring ladies down at the test barn.

"You rinse that?" Marv asked as he poured about a quarter of the bottle of bigeloil into half a bucket of water.

"It's new," I said.

"Get it wet," he said, flick of the wrist, index finger pointing toward the hose.

I rinsed the sponge, wrung it out, Marv growing impatient, one quick circle with the hand.

"Come on, Bass." I handed him the sponge, round side up, the way you hold it, same as the hoof pick, hoof knife, pincers, and rasp when he was under the horse, holding a leg up, shoeing.

I took a trip backward in time, remembering when we would be out shoeing horses on a Saturday. There was a system, and we followed it. We handed him the tools by the handle, goddamnit, by the handle, in order, and don't make him wait. Hand him the heavy pincers and he would peel off a horse-shoe to be re-used, the nails filed with a rasp. He woud hand my brother or me the shoe, and with a chisel we bought him for Christmas at that cool little hardware store in Lacrosse, we'd remove the nails. Hold the shoe and chisel on the anvil in one hand, hit it hard and clip the nail, lay it upside down flat, and line the nail up over the round hole in the big Peter Wright anvil. It was a heavy anvil, seventy-some pounds of solid steel. Punch the nails through, a pass or two from the old wire brush, hand it to Marv as he handed you the rasp, take it with the left hand as you hand him the shoe with the right.

He places the shoe on the hoof, tilts his head a little, that cowboy hat, the old gray sweat-stained felt, more glove than hat, low crown and age curled brim. It fits him pretty well and sticks with him from sunup to sundown as he makes a quick assessment, drops the hoof and approaches the anvil, pulled all the way to the edge of the tailgate of the green Ford f250. The point of the anvil out over the edge of the tailgate and straight, goddamnit, straight.

Hand him the two-pound ball peen hammer, round on one end. He uses the flat side to shape the shoe, the round end to get the kinks out, back to the flat end to level the shoe. Quick swig of water out of the mason jar, and back to the side of the horse. He stands at the horse's shoulder, glances toward the horizon as he runs his hand down the horse's leg to his ankle, squeezes a little and the horse lifts his foot.

A good horse, not working him over too much, the shoe in Marv's left hand. He sizes it up one more time, drops the hoof gently, back to the anvil, two shots with the big hammer. He takes a long drink this time, a vee-shaped sweat stain forming on his back, wet and getting wider, just about to his belt, the sun getting lower in the sky and two to go after this one.

He grabs a handful of nails, does that himself, gets them all pointed the same way, head in. Nine pointed nails in his mouth, shoe in his left hand, runs his hand from the shoulder to the ankle, squeeze, lift. I hand him the ten-ounce shoeing hammer, wooden handle, claw on one end. He cups the hoof in his hand, the nails appearing between the space in his fingers as he taps them through the hoof wall, low, so you don't "quick" the hoof, drive the nail into the tender part. Four nails on each side of the shoe, all in a straight row, straight, goddamnit, straight, twisting the ends of the nail off as he goes. About five taps with the hammer for each nail, three soft and two hard, flip the hammer, twist the nail, snatch another nail out of his mouth, adjust his feet, and repeat seven more times.

"Here, ya son of a bitch," he says to the horse, the nails clenched in his teeth. "Wiggle his head," he says to the holder.

Hand him the block, he holds it firm against the nails on the outside of the hoof with his right hand, drives the nails all the way home with a final smack of the hammer in his left hand. From the top, eight nails, eight swings of the hammer, he drops the block and hands me his hammer. He swings the hoof forward as I hand him the clincher, he clinches the nails, I take the clincher and hand him the rasp, he gives it one final pass over the hoof wall.

Do it all one more time on the back leg and sell that son of a bitch, go get that bay right there.

Maybe crack open the first Budweiser of the day between horses, while Deke gets the bay. This one is skinny enough to come back with an offer, a good candidate for the program, probably get him for seventy-five, cash. Make a quick five hundred if you can put a rein on him, three hundred if not.

Marv wipes a little dust off Officer's Citation's back, says "Whoa, Provee," and drops the sponge in the bucket. "Bass," he says, bringing me back to 1987.

"Yeah?"

"Soak that sponge, get him damp from the withers all the way up over his ass, shoulders too,'" Marv said, "Then put that

213

cooler on, get him damp, not wet." Draws a figure eight in the air. "Hand me your Wall Street."

"Got one for you over on the straw."

I usually bought two racing forms.

I can smell the bigeloil as I ease the blanket over his back, and adjust it, straight, goddamnit, straight.

We walk up to the cafe, Marv gets a coffee, I get a coke, and we catch the seven o'clock local news update as we head for a table by the wall. Marv sees me crack a smile as I see the news anchor.

"The hell you grinning about?"

Waving vaguely at the tv, I say, "Met his sister at the Stock-yards last night."

"Might not be the only one in this town knows her," he said, shrugging his shoulders, just a little.

"Close to fame as I ever been."

"Only worth bragging about if it's as close as you're ever gonna get," he said, the gentlest reminder I ever had to stay humble.

"You asked."

"You ain't gotta answer every thing's asked," he said, driving the nail home with one final smack of the hammer.

We sat down to wait for Baldy to arrive. He arrived a few minutes later, and we were back at the barn by eight, there for good tonight. A quick trip to the rail to watch the race, then we come back, quiet, going easy around the stall.

Officer's Citation has his head out of the stall now, his ears pricked forward, pretty as a picture, the white cooler stained a little now. He's got a pretty good sweat going.

"Too much bigeloil, you can blister them," Marv says. "'Bout two ounces to the gallon is all you want on a night like this." Still hot at the end of August, about seventy-five degrees this late, but cooling down pretty quick as it does at night in the Pacific Northwest. Might bottom out around sixty, cool enough to sleep.

They just called the eighth to the receiving barn, not too long to wait now, getting closer, the horse acting good, nice and relaxed. Sixth coming off the track at the gap, seventh in the saddling paddock, eighth in the receiving barn as the horses from the hole who finished up the track make their way back to the stable, the groom sometimes with his head down, sometimes up, depending on whether it was third, or further back.

"How'd you come back?" you hear a horseman ask, and don't catch the reply.

The same voice asks, "Where you end up?"

"Nowhere," says the groom, subdued. He's wondering if they are going to get it figured out. He's walking by with a tired horse, headed for a solitary yellow lamp glimmering in the distance, and a quiet stall down in the hole.

The first two finishers peel off to the test barn, and you know they don't feel too bad, no matter which horse they've got. You can usually tell who the winner is by the spring in the step of horse and groom alike.

Nearly everyone on the backstretch has faced nearly every emotion that comes with the official order of finish. Given the chance, they will all try again tomorrow if fortune and fate allow them another day on the backstretch.

Horses for the ninth race are called to the receiving barn. There is a little activity now as we get the entire stable ready for his race. One final pick of the hooves, card the mane and tail, put the bridle on, forelock over the top of the forehead band.

Most people tuck the forelock under the band, but I like to

think my horse can run fast enough for the wind to keep the forelock out of his eyes. It looks better out, anyway.

Noise from the grandstand, and it's finally time. Soak the sponge, peel the cooler, wring the sponge out over his back, replace the cooler with the good black one, line up the bottom edges even, get them straight, goddamnit, straight.

"Attention horsemen, bring your horses to the receiving barn for the tenth race. Horses to the receiving barn for the tenth."

Marv says, "Wait."

You hear only one set of hooves coming up from the hole tonight, and see a familiar chestnut horse, see a familiar face.

"God damn, Darrell, one of us gotta run through." Marv says.

Darrell taps his horse on the shoulder, points to mine, says, "That son of a bitch right there," and says to Marv, "Look like us if you kill the speed, partner."

Marv gives his head that one shake, wearing a good white straw hat tonight, a little higher crown than the brown or grey, the curved brim just like it was coming out of the box, squeezed a little narrower in the front by Marv. He's not saying, either way, and says, "he's liable to run off with the bug, but I ain't sure we got horse enough to hook 'im and live to tell the tale."

"Time will tell, I reckon," says a little bit of a southern accent, but the program says he's from Kennewick. "Good luck, men," says Darrell, Marv giving me the flick and I fall in behind the good looking little chestnut, honest enough, but about a length behind us every time so far.

"Right there," says Darrell, as we make our way to the receiving barn, looking to graduate tonight with our horses, both chestnut and brown. "Just keep 'im right there."

We arrive at the receiving barn, and quick as a wink, Marv's got the headstall number on. "Stand him in the stall, if he will."

I give him a quick circuit of the small paddock, take him in and head him out of the stall. My back is to Officer's Citation's chest on the left side, his head over my shoulder as we stand quietly and survey the competition, my little brown Thoroughbred and I. I reach back with my right hand, scratch him on the neck on the off side, look at the horse dropping in, a good looking bay, and I say to my horse, "He ain't got Citation for a grandpappy, kiddo."

Officer's Citation nods, not voicing an opinion, acknowledging the fact.

We hear the crowd, then the PA barks, "Attention, horsemen, please bring your horses to the paddock for the tenth race, horses to the paddock for the tenth," and we are headed around the north end once again, on the now familiar pavement, starting to remember where even the cracks in the pavement lie and to where they lead.

I ask again, where else would you rather be?

Like walking on a cloud, the surface good tonight, we wait a minute for the tractors to get around the turn, the diesel smoke lingering in the air, slowly settling as we continue to the paddock.

I see the wrist flick, and to the stall we go, head out. Marv peels the cooler as I slip the reins, buckled together at the barn, over Officer's Citation's head, and we make the turn in the back of the stall. Get him stopped heading out, work the bit, lean against him as they tighten the girth and he comes up on his toes. Then back on the move for two circuits, and maybe one more. As we pass the stall as Lightfoot says, "Riders out," and we keep walking as he gives it a minute, and says "Put your horses in please." We take a wide path as I try not to pass the slowpoke in front of me before I get to the stall.

"One," says Lightfoot, the bugler sounds the call to post, and we execute our part in the rhythm that is the exchange of racehorses between groom and pony at the paddock gap.

I'm done and off the track, down the steps, up and into the snake pit.

I watch the race with Carol. There is an honest pace to run down, and the two front runners are weakening at the quarter pole. Officer's Citation takes the first run at them, and he is in front by a length at the eighth pole, but Margos Flag is inching closer.

A sixteenth to go now, Officer's Citation is trying to hang on, and it looks like he will. Margos Flag is still coming, but it looks like he is going to run out of real estate. The two horses hit the wire together, but it looks to me like we are a head in front at the finish. We begin to migrate to the winner's circle. My hands are shaking.

The horses run through together, pull up together, and jog back to the winner's circle together. Margos Flag has his ears pricked forward, Officer's Citation is switching his forward and back, the first indication I had that he may not have won. It didn't appear that Officer's Citation thought he had won.

The sign on the tote board said "Photo Finish", and the numbers six and eight are flashing. The lights go out, the sign stops flashing, and the numbers appear again, this time in reverse order, the eight first, and the six second. The sign flashes, "official."

Damn it.

It was official, and we were second by a nose. It was very close, but it is the difference between breaking even and cashing a decent ticket. For the horse, it was the difference between eight hundred eighty dollars, and three hundred twenty. It was close, but we were second. Nailed on the money.

Damn it. That one hurt.

We climb the steps and walk through the winner's circle to pick up an honest little brown Thoroughbred who just missed.

"Still got our conditions, Darrell, where'd you end up?" Marv asks, as we lean on the rail and watch our horses gallop back to the wire.

"Right behind you, Marv, but a little more distant in the rearview, this time," says Darrell. "I reckon we'll try 'em again."

"Looks that way," Marv says, as I pick up the horse and notice the girl from the test barn give my horse a pat on the shoulder after she clips the tag on his bridle.

"You gonna let me out before last call tonight?" she asks her little brown Thoroughbred, giving him a scratch on his neck. He didn't answer.

We headed for the test barn, and she and I both missed last call. It was probably just as well, I had a truckload of straw waiting for me in the morning before I would reluctantly head back to the farm after the races.

Cutting Back

A gray horse leading them to the wire.

Six days later, we wheeled back and cut the distance back to one mile.

We would be in the fifth race, the last time we would run in a race that was not the nightcap.

A horse cutting back in distance will usually be pretty tough in the stretch, and we were hoping to gain an advantage this way.

It was a pretty uneventful week on the farm, but I had to leave early Friday night, so I parked the machine at four thirty or so, on a beautiful sunny Friday, right in the middle of harvest, pleasing no one and not very worried about it

Milt said, "Sooner or later, you're gonna have to decide between those horses and work."

"I'm ready to decide as soon as you need me to."

"See you Monday," he said, not very enthusiastically. Probably couldn't understand why anyone would want to leave the farm, while I couldn't see why anyone would want to stay.

I was leaving, one way or the other, even before the horse came along. The summer of 1987 was when the choice became clear, and I was as surprised as anyone that the deciding factor had something to do with horses.

But it did, and he was in tonight.

I took highway one ninety-five north to Spokane, zipped by the apartment for a quick shower and change of clothes, and arrived about six-fifteen. I saw the first race on the monitor at the cafe as I went through to pick up a program and a form.

"Bass," said Marv, as I approached the stall. "Didn't know if you were going to make it."

I raised my eyebrows a bit, wondering where else he might think I would be.

"You drag up?" he said, asking if I quit the farm.

"Not yet. I think we'll probably make it official in another week. Much more, and that hundred a day is gonna bankrupt the farm."

"Doin' them a favor," Marv said, playing along.

"Seems like the least I can do."

Through the next few years, from Oregon to British Columbia, Marv came to be more surprised when I missed a race, no matter how far I had to drive, than when I made it.

Nothing much was happening at the barn. Officer's Citation was standing with his head out the door, his ears pricked forward. I gave him a scratch on the neck. "How's the big hoss?" I asked no one in particular.

"On his toes," said Marv. "You seen the Wall Street?"

"Just picked one up," I said.

"Picked all over the place, the rotten sonsabitches," Marv said.

Marv used to write a handicapping sheet for the track in Coeur D' Alene, usually touting the lesser horses so he could get a good price on the better horses. He usually took it both as a source of pride and a personal insult when his horse was picked to win.

I leaned against the chains, the bruise literally a fading memory, and cracked open the form to the first race. Officer's Citation put his head over my shoulder to assist in the handicapping.

Sure enough, we were picked first or second by all the handicappers. A horse named Rodeo Purple was dropping in, a late closer who looked like he would be tough. We might be able to steal it on the front end, but it looked like there was enough cheap speed entered that we would have a pace to target. Which meant, so would the other horse. It looked pretty even on paper.

There was nothing else in worth worrying about, all horses who Officer's Citation had previously outrun in one race or another. No Butterfield tonight, either.

The second race went, and Marv and I watched it from the rail. Third to the paddock, Fourth to the receiving barn; time to get the horse ready. No sweat required today, his back was a lot better after a visit from the equine chiropractor. We heard the cheer build and fade from the grandstand, and could hear the muted pa system on the grandstand side.

"Attention horsemen, please bring your horses to the receiving barn for the fifth race. Horses to the receiving barn for the fifth."

My heart leaped into my throat a little like it did the first time this announcement ever pertained to me, and nearly every time since.

Marv said, "Wait."

You might think it wasn't necessary for him to say this every time we heard the call, but he did. I hated being late, left over from waiting in the car before school for a sister who insisted on being twenty minutes late for every occasion, no matter what. I was usually twenty minutes early if I had any control over when I arrived. It was very necessary for him to tell me to wait.

A few minutes later, he said, "Okay, Bass," and I led my little brown Thoroughbred out of the stall, took a right in the shedrow, and another right on the paved pathway to the receiving barn.

Officers Citation was moving so lightly, I could barely feel him as I led him by the reins, the way Marv had shown me. I wasn't leading him, so much as I was walking with him to the receiving barn. He knew the way as well as I did. We stopped for a moment as the winner of the third crossed our path going to the test barn.

The young lady from the test barn, the one who didn't like to stay late, saw us. "Hey, I might get out of here on time tonight," she said, smiling.

"Maybe."

"See ya in a little bit," she said, assuming we would be in the test barn later this evening.

"Got a fan club, I see," Marv said, giving the horse a pat on the neck. He had the headstall number on before I knew it was in his hand. "Give him a turn, Bass. Well, hell, you know what to do, I'll see you over there." He walked off toward the gap. I stood Officer's Citation in the stall, head out, and watched Rodeo Purple walk calmly around the small paddock.

"That one, right there," I said to my horse. He nodded but didn't seem impressed.

We heard the cheers rise and fall from the grandstand in the distance. It gave me a little chill then, it gives me a little chill remembering it just now.

"Attention, horsemen, please bring your horses to the paddock for the fifth race. Horses to the paddock for the fifth." My heart slammed into my throat, on schedule.

Officer's Citation was completely relaxed, heading for the paddock for the sixth time that year, but the damp spots would have been appearing on my flanks, as I was starting to wash out a little. I was agitated, still, from hurrying up from the farm. I hadn't been able to settle down, but I was trying to keep my hands off my horse, lest I transfer the nerves to him.

No worries there, though, at least one of us was acting like a professional. We walked around the north end, and I led my horse in a lazy zigzag, trying to stay behind the horse in front of us.

As we entered the track from the six and a half furlong chute, Officer's Citation took a lunge forward, kicked with both hind feet, gathered himself and continued walking like nothing had happened. I was ready for him and still couldn't feel him at the end of the reins. He was right where we wanted him.

We were among the first saddled, in and out of the stall so quick it didn't seem like we were there at all. A few circuits, riders out, riders up, take the horse to the pony, head to the snake pit and slam a drink. I bet twenty across the board, a twenty dollar exacta box with my horse and Rodeo Purple. I paid with a hundred, collected my ticket, and spent my last five dollars on another Seven and Seven. I took a little time sipping it, watching the warm-ups on the closed circuit monitor above the bar.

I wandered out to the bench to watch the race with my aunt and uncle.

"Bass," said Baldy. "They let you out of rehab?"

"Haven't caught me yet."

"How's your horse?"

"He's good," I said. "Groom's a little washy, though."

He gritted his teeth and nodded, "How you see it?"

"That purple shitter looks a little tough," I said.

Baldy gritted his teeth, nodded.

I wandered to the rail to watch the race, standing across from the sixteenth pole, in front of the tote board. The gate was loaded quickly.

The PA crackled to life, "Flag is up, all in line."

"There they go!"

The butterflies in my stomach do a final dance, then disappear.

Officer's Citation gets away good, settles in about sixth, Rodeo Purple seventh, matching the numbers on their saddle cloths, six and seven, Rodeo Purple a length or two back. They round the clubhouse turn, into the backstretch and Officer's Citation begins to pass horses as they go past the three-eighths, running three wide and taking a length lead at the three-sixteenths, turning for home two in front. Something was running late, looked kind of like a big gray horse. He was coming through on the rail, then veering to the outside of Officer's Citation, gaining as they passed the eighth pole. Rodeo Purple went by Officer's Citation at the sixteenth, and a horse named Rich Pass came running late and we dead-heated for second place with him.

The numbers flash, and I get back about sixty dollars on my hundred dollar bet. At least I could afford a beer tonight, and could pick up a few bucks working for Rizzuto this weekend.

I lead a dejected horse to the test barn, kicking bark the whole way. I would have kicked rocks, but I never saw very many walking across the infield at Playfair, ever.

"I knew you'd come see me today," said the young lady at the test barn to my horse. She noticed the air was kind of heavy, and asked me, "What happened?"

I held up two fingers, said, "Second again."

"Oh, you're such a good boy, you try so hard," she said, getting carried away, patting my horse on both sides of his neck. "Let's get you shampooed."

So I give him some water, he got another free bath, and we waited in the test barn for the sample. It eventually trickled out after another three hours, and just as the last horse from the tenth race exited the test barn.

"Just barely," said the young lady, whose name was still a mystery to me. "Still last one out, but at least we made it on time."

"See you next time," I said, proud of my horse.

Still got our conditions, I thought, as we headed for the barn.

The Door

Hoist the Flag, grandsire of Officer's Citation

Six races in the books, $1925 in earnings, or an average of $320 per start, up from $156 per start last year. We had enough of the calendar left for three more starts, maybe four, all of it depending on his health. Officer's Citation had earned more in six starts in 1987 than he had earned in twelve starts in 1986.

The next morning, he was a tired horse, and I felt some heat in his left knee. Not much, but it was there. We would check it every day, and assess the situation on a daily basis. He had

228

cleaned up his feed, but he was not nearly as aggressive about going after it this morning.

We cut his feed again the next evening, only giving him the ration he had cleaned up the previous night.

I ran cold water on his knees and ankles, about fifteen minutes each, the morning after the race, but there was no swelling, and he wasn't limping. It looked like we were okay, but time would tell.

Sunday morning, he was going after the feed, and the heat in his knee was gone. He was still tired, still had dark circles around his eyes, but he was coming around.

I didn't work Sunday, just did the chores in the morning and hung out for a while at the rail. Not nearly as much training was going on, just a trainer or two in the guinea stand. I hung out on the backstretch until noon, mostly cleaning or just loafing around the barn, and walked over to watch Saturdays replays.

I watched a few races, hit the daily double for the only time in my life, and collected on a ten dollar ticket, the short-priced favorites winning their respective races in the first two. The winner in the first was Mountain Goose, the winner in the second was Big Time Moose. Wildlife was well represented, but it sure didn't pay much. Marv told me on the phone to bet the goose to the moose in the daily double. I broke even on the day, maybe a little better.

By this time, I knew the horses pretty well. The horses who had graduated in front of Officer's Citation were holding their own in the open races at the bottom. It both gave and put a ceiling on the hope I had for my horse.

I fed my horse, and went back to the apartment to get some sleep so I could be on the road by four-thirty next morning, headed back to the farm for at least another week.

Next morning, at about a quarter to six, I was riding the Yamaha through the town of Thornton, on the way to the farm. The place I worked had an office on the corner, and Milt's red and white Ford was parked outside.

The office was just a small trailer, and I went up the four steps, knocked twice, and Milt opened the door.

"Morning," I said.

"Hey, kid," he said, usually a good sign, kid. "Come on in, have a seat. You want some coffee?"

The hell was going on, here?

"I'll get it." I poured a cup, sat down in front of his desk as he was writing something. "What's up?"

He finished writing with a sort of a flourish, and I had a pretty good idea what was up, but I had never been that lucky, so I waited without feeling much one way or the other.

"I think we can get by without you, from here on in," said Milt. He handed me a check.

I had worked twenty-two days, had a check in my hand for twenty-five hundred dollars. Milt had lectured us many times, when you wanted to get rid of someone, pay them more than they are owed and show them the door.

I stuck out my hand, shook his, and said, "I know where the door is."

I don't recall saying anything else, and I think that was the last time I was ever in the town of Thornton.

It took me about an hour to get back to Spokane, and I was walking into the backstretch cafe by seven o'clock in the morning.

Bill Rizzuto was at one of the tables, and he looked up as I walked in. "Thought you were going south today?" he said.

"Quick trip," I said. "I could use a day off, but I'm available starting tomorrow unless you really need something today."

Bill said, "You done harvesting?"

"Oh, yeah," I said.

"We're good today, I'll see you in the morning," he said, pausing a moment. "Everything OK?"

"Yeah," I said. "Everything is good."

I believed it. It was good. I walked down, fed my horse, didn't notice any heat in his knee, or anywhere else.

I looked at the straw in his stall. I thought about the wheat straw, same stuff exactly, during the harvest, in the field. I thought about clearing the wheat straw, bound together with morning glory, out of the back of a combine, hot, dusty, itchy, and one handful at a time. I thought about cleaning the stall, wheat straw soaked with urine. I could either be in an air-conditioned cab this morning, or pitching horse shit at the race track. It was an easy choice, and a very good day.

I put my horse on the walker and went for the wheelbarrow, already three hours into the best Monday I had in nearly a month. I bet they still don't pay a hundred a day down on the farm.

The week passed, and I celebrated my twenty-second birthday that Tuesday. I don't remember it, so it was either an epic drunk, or relatively uneventful, possibly both. Good things usually don't happen to me on my birthday, in fact it is usually the opposite. Uneventful was okay with me.

Finally, race day arrived, Saturday, September 12, 1987.

I stripped the stall, removed the hay net, pulled the water bucket, and tried to pass some time.

Officer's Citation had cleaned up his breakfast in five minutes. I skipped mine. All systems were go.

I actually even asked Bill if he was sure he didn't need

anything. He didn't, and I ended up raking the walking ring. I even cleaned and organized the tack room.

I walked up to the cafe, studied the form. It still looked like it was going to be tough.

I drove over to the Flame, a dark and seedy restaurant and lounge on the corner of Sprague and Altamont, the closest bar to the track, and a regular hangout for a lot of racetrackers. It was pretty quiet this afternoon. I drank a bottle of Budweiser, studied the form. It didn't look any easier under the dim lights in the lounge at the Flame.

I walked down the street to the Double Clutch, another dive, this time with pool tables and fried chicken to go, so I got a box of chicken, drank a Budweiser, and studied the form.

Didn't look much easier from under the dim lights of the Double Clutch.

A few trackers were drinking, playing pool, killing time. We nodded to each other. I had another beer, another piece of chicken, studied the form.

It was about four thirty when I went back to the track.

It really was pretty routine until we got to the paddock, where it was still pretty routine, except for one thing.

First, the tactical situation: We were cutting back to six and a half furlongs, and we were facing horses who had been sprinting. The claiming price was $5000, and the condition was never won three. It was the toughest race we had entered, but cutting back in distance would give us a legitimate chance, provided the race didn't come up too tough.

With an apprentice jockey, this would have put us in at 117 pounds, and I can't imagine Baldy not trying for a five-pound pull going a mile, but the unusual thing was that we had a rider who could only do 122, sometimes not even that. So we were in at 122 no matter what the form said.

His name was Mike Baze, and he was a good rider. Had a few demons, like so many on the backstretch. Frankly, the only way you got a rider like Mike at a small track like Playfair was on the way up, or on the way down. Or on the bounce, as they ricocheted off rock bottom.

So on the bounce, Mike was having a good season, either first or second in the standings. I'm pretty sure he would have been first, but he was having a few problems, still, and would find himself suspended for one reason or another about once a month.

However it happened, Mike rode the horse.

Officer's Citation was feeling good that night, and I had my hands full of horse. I was also feeling good that night. I thought Mike was a hell of a rider, because he was. It was in his pedigree. We were saddled quickly, and I was watching Marv as I led the horse in wide circles around the paddock as slowly as I could get him to walk.

Lightfoot called for riders, and I headed to the stall. I got there when Mike arrived, in time to hear the instructions Marv had for him. It was even money as to whether or not instructions were ever followed, but they were usually given at any rate.

Marv says, "Now, Mike…"

Mike says, "Shh." Listens for the call, riders up. Listens intently for about ten seconds of silence.

Marv looks at the ground, may have been a tiny shake of the head, just one. Looks over at Mike, starts to speak, Mike holds up a finger, raises his eyebrows, listens for the signal.

"Riders up!"

I thought Marv might throw him out of the stall when he legged Mike up. I'm a little surprised he didn't.

The thing is, the race came up pretty tough, and the best result anyone could see was second place, including everyone at the barn, and a few of the handicappers for the Daily Racing Form. We were probably the fourth best horse in the race. If the rider would have just pretended to be courteous, all would have been forgiven.

I'm pretty sure Mike had won a riding title or two at Longacres, but Mike hadn't been anywhere Marv and Baldy hadn't. He didn't get there first, either. So, it was what it was, and it wasn't about tactics.

The horses approached the starting gate, and I couldn't really tell, but he was acting good and walked right into the starting gate. The six and a half furlong chute is basically a sixteenth of a mile extension at the head of the home stretch, and that is where the race started. There were five horses with a chance, but the truth is, four of them, including us, were running for second. Unless someone wanted to nominate his horse for a suicide mission, we were running for second.

Marv wanted to race accordingly, get a little further back early, make a shorter, faster run late, and maybe pass a few tiring horses and finish second, first if we get really lucky.

Nobody really knew what Mike thought, other than it was really important for a rider to hear the paddock judge say "Riders up."

So they're all in the gate. There they go, and in order around the clubhouse turn and into the backstretch, it's grey, chestnut, bay, brown, miscellaneous. We are running fourth, the third best horse is third, second best is second, and the legitimate speed horse, a sprinter routing, is alone on the lead.

The margins get wider, but no horses change positions. They are a bit strung out, and we finish an uninspiring fourth place, seven lengths behind the winner. Anyone could have seen it coming. It is possible no one could have changed the result, very possible.

What was impossible, was seeing Mike ride another horse for M.D. Putzier in the near future. At least, it wasn't anything they were going to discuss tonight.

The horses crossed the finish line, pulled up, turned around, and made a nice easy medium gallop back to the finish line. The jockeys dismounted, and with some help from the valets, unsaddle the horses.

I waved, Mike saw me, steered the horse our way, and jogged to a walk and then a stop.

Mike was a bit more talkative. "They just didn't come back to me," He said as he slid off the horse and his feet hit the ground. He unhooked the overgirth, unhooked the girth, turned to Marv and said, "I'll ride him back."

You could see it this time, that one shake. It looked like they made eye contact for a moment or two.

Mike, a little wide-eyed now, looked at me as I was holding the horse.

I raised my eyebrows. Doesn't look like it.

So, one start, one fourth, fifty-five dollars. Lifetime statistics for the Marvin Putzier / Mike Baze trainer/ jockey combo.

He wasn't breathing that hard, Officer's Citation. We walked down the track to the gap, across the infield, and I leaned into him as I turned Officer's Citation to the right, away from the test barn, and toward the stable.

It was the first time I had to give him a bath in a month. We cooled him out, and cut him back a half can of oats but expected no problems. The race was essentially nothing more than a three-quarter mile long work. I did his legs up with medicated mud and bedded him down with fresh straw. We would see what tomorrow would bring.

The Four-Footed Industry

Joe Gottstein, founder of Longacres Racetrack in Renton,
Washington, near Seattle.

Officer's Citation was a tired horse the next morning, but his
legs and knees were cold. He didn't have a mark on him, and
he went right to the feed tub after I re-acquainted myself with
the shampooing procedure. He did the best he could, and as

238

usual, he knew it.

He was going to get two weeks off, and not go to the track at all if we could help it.

In the meantime, as a promotional event, a celebrity was coming to town, and his name was Bill Shoemaker.

Shoemaker was on the downside of a career that had made him the best rider in the nation for several years running. He had won the previous years Kentucky Derby aboard Ferdinand. He was still among the best riders in the nation when he rode the promotional race at Playfair in 1987.

"How the hell they get him up here to ride the bullring?" Baldy wondered aloud.

They did, however, and he rode the favorite in the featured race. Baldy and I watched the race from the rail by the guinea stand. It must have been run at a mile or a mile and a sixteenth because the start was on the backstretch. He was on the nine-horse, I do remember that.

I figured he would show the local riders a thing or two about being on the rail around the turn. It is difficult to convince a rider that they lose ground on the turns when they are outside, but they do. Run an entire race four wide, and come back and say, "You've got a short horse."

While bad races are always the jockeys fault, and while they always should have gone through that hole on the rail, it should be pointed out that it takes a large amount of courage to be a race-rider. Six inches away from an immovable rail on a live Thoroughbred with horses all around you running nearly forty miles an hour is not for the faint of heart.

It sure wasn't looking good for Shoe as they went into the far turn for the first time, however. He was four wide, and they were pretty well into the turn. And then, faster than you can say, "Wow," he was on the rail, and moving to the front of the horses who were inside him just a second ago. He just lifted that horse's head, turned him to the inside, and was on the rail. It was something to see. He squirted up to about fifth as they passed the grandstand for the first time, and kept a head in front of the horse outside, close to getting trapped on the rail, but a head too fast for them.

Down the backstretch and into the final turn, he kept them outside, and when the leader hit the quarter pole, Shoemaker and his horse surged forward, scraped paint along the rail out of the turn, and easily passed the collapsing front runners to win the race. It was a masterful ride. Shoemaker was still signing autographs as the fans drifted out after the races. It was pretty cool to see the master at work.

Shoe went back to California, and we went back to our one horse stable. We weren't going to ask our horse to do anything for the next ten days.

In the course of loafing around and lighting cigarettes for Baldy, and hanging around on the backstretch with him and Marv, the subject of companion animals came up.

Dogs are usually not allowed on the backstretch, but cats, even black ones, are for some reason allowed.

The most common companion animal in the stall with the horse is, of course, the goat.

Marv didn't like goats. We had a variety of animals growing up, and none of them were ugly, ever. They were always a great representative of whatever breed or species they were. Beautiful is not a word you hear applied to goats, much. I always figured it was a simple as that, but it was not.

Marv was a horse trader, and so was Baldy. Sometime in the sixties, a race they were in had just finished running, and they were out to pick up the horse as he came back to the wire. Baldy spoke to one of his friends, a trainer with a horse in the same race.

"Where'd you come out, Jim?" asked Baldy.

Jim said, "Up the track." Nowhere close. "How about you?"

"Up the track," said Baldy. "How about we trade, who you got?"

"This little bay coming right here," Jim said, "Who you got?"

"That son of a bitch in the white silks, the seven," said Baldy, as the jock and valet unsaddled the bay.

Jim shrugged his shoulders, and handed the reins and the horse to Baldy. Baldy began to walk back to the stable area leading his new horse. He thought of something and turned to Marv.

"I never cleared this with you," Baldy said.

"I never asked who you had, either," said Marv, happy to trade horses, always.

So they get the horse back to the barn, and later Jim and his wife came over to the stable leading a goat.

"Hey, Baldy," Jim said, "that horse doesn't go anywhere without the goat, the two are inseparable. They love each other."

Marv and Baldy, noticing how skinny and poor the horse was, figure it can't hurt, at least until they get to know the quirks of the horse a little better. They accept the goat, feed the horse and put the goat in the stall with him.

"I come back to the stall," Baldy said, "and that god damned goat was head=butting the horse, wouldn't let him into the feed tub to eat."

Marv said, "We gave the goat away, and I'll be damned if we didn't fatten that horse up and have a decent trade on our hands."

"Shoulda slit his throat," Baldy said. "So we get the sono-fabitch up to a race, figure we had a gamble set up."

"Morning of the race, he's got a knot on his neck the size of a golf ball," Marv said.

"What happened?" I asked.

"I think somebody tried to help us, or hurt us, I was never sure which," Baldy said.

"What was it?" I asked.

"Turned out to be cancer," Baldy said. "But whatever it was started that day, with a syringe full of who-knows-what. We sold that son of a bitch to a chicken farmer for two hundred."

"And happy to get it," said Marv.

"Jesus," said Baldy, shaking his head at the memory.

"Goats," Marv said, shaking his head. "Bad as mules, you ask me."

So they didn't all work out. The only part of that story I never believed was that they didn't know the horse they had traded for. They didn't miss much, either of them.

Scouting the county with Marv one lazy spring day, we passed a herd of mules in one of those backroad pastures along a winding gravel road we traveled occasionally on our scouting trips.

"Fucking mules," Marv said quietly, deep into an ancient memory. "Huh, Bass."

"Yeah," I said. I had a little experience with mules, and I found them to be neither majestic not inspirational. I think it was more personal with Marv, though.

There were some characters who would drop by the barn, the good friends, the drinking buddies. One of them was Sam Tilden, normally a very reserved and polite man, big, probably tacked two thirty or so, pretty solid. He came by one day and got into a story about when he was down at the Double Clutch, one of the dive bars on Sprague Avenue near the track, and a couple of law officers came in with a warrant for his arrest.

"They come in, the bulls do, two of them," Sam said, "and one of 'em said, 'Mister Tilden, we have a warrant for your arrest.' So I take a drink of my beer, don't say anything, and they each take a step closer, one on each side. One of 'em says, 'can we do this the easy way?'" Sam chuckled a little as he continued. " I set my glass down, and I said, 'Earn your money, you sonsabitches,' and we tangled a little bit. They beat the hell out of me eventually, but we were a pretty rough looking bunch by the time we got to jail."

"Sammy was an orangutan," Marv said, watching him walk away. "He could fight."

Baldy spent most of the years training horses, having success at tracks in California, Oregon and Washington. He also pulled a pretty major upset at Longacres in Seattle, ruining the end of a promotional film the owner of Longacres had put together.

Somewhere out there in the piles of lost film and video is a video made for promotional purposes in the late fifties or sixties called, "The Four-Footed Industry." It was made by or commissioned by Joe Gottstein, or his son in law, Morris Alhadeff, one or the other. Joe was the owner and founder of Longacres, in the Seattle area.

I don't know or remember exactly how it went, but the essence was that they followed a horse, owned by whoever commissioned the film, from his training, all the way up to the day of the big race. Then came the race, in which the promoted horse was the heavy favorite. The race was the climactic scene in the promotional film.

I'll let Marv finish telling the story.

"That son of a bitch Baldy was training, (he named the horse), ran past Gottstein's horse at the sixteenth pole, won the race," Marv said. "The last thing you see is Baldy leading him into the winner's circle."

I bet they got a nice price.

For some reason, no one ever gets back to me when I inquire about this film. I painted a house for one of the Alhadeffs, I think his name was Mike. He and I talked a lot about horse racing and horses, but I don't recall the movie ever being acknowledged when I tried to bring it up. Mike was a very nice man, very kind and good to me. The truth is, he may not have known about the film. He may not have heard me ask, either.

I'm not trying to infer anything one way or the other, I'm just saying no one seems to know where I can see it, and other than Marv or Baldy, no one seems to want to talk very much about it.

We walked Officer's Citation between races, not going to the track at all until the morning of the race. Then we went once around real slow, just to take the edge off a little. We gave him some additional vitamin B supplements to "pick his head up," as Marv put it. They called it "hanging a jug on them," as it was actually an intravenous drip type container from which these supplements were delivered to the bloodstream for many years. The horse was coming around. His legs were back under him, he was sound and starting to feel good again. The jug would help.

We were at the quarter pole of the season, three races to go. I liked the walk for the nightcap when the backstretch was quiet as we led our horses through the stable area. It was about ten o'clock at night, fifteen minutes to post for the tenth race, Saturday, September 26, 1987 as we made our way through the stable area on the north side of Playfair.

I led a tough and relaxed horse to the paddock, and the race looked a little tricky on the form. The problem was, there was a lone speed horse in the race, but he was not a better horse than the one I was leading. Marv decided to hook him.

Marv intended to force the cheap speed horse into a faster pace than he wanted. Marv figured we could put him away on the front end in less than a half mile, and still get the win, as we were picked all over the form to win, and had a tough horse. We were running a mile and a sixteenth.

And Officer's Citation got it done, cooked the speed, and hit the quarter pole in front by a length. Trouble is, they don't pay at the quarter pole. He was fourth at the eighth pole, seventh at the finish. The horse he hooked finished ninth, but there was no payoff for winning a suicide pact with another horse. Everyone shoots themselves. It was his worst race that year, and he looked great for seven furlongs. It was not a good feeling, watching your horse go backward in the stretch.

I led a sore and tired horse back to the barn, both our heads hanging low, subdued, humble. I've led a lot of losers back to the barn, and some of them don't change much, third or worse. I got the feeling my little brown Thoroughbred was depressed, though, almost heartbroken. He didn't believe there was a horse at our level who could beat him, and he was choking on his humility, same as I. I gave him a warm bath, went back with him through his pedigree, and tried to prop him up, see what I could do for his self-esteem.

He was hurting, and the vet was called. The vet gave him a shot of the painkiller Butazolidin, directly into the bloodstream. This took effect quickly, and it was a quiet barn as we cooled our horse out.

I cut him back to a half ration of feed, and exchanged the cooler on his back for a light, dry cooler. I had lost a hundred dollars on the race and didn't think about it until I turned out the light after picking up my form in the tack room. I was worried about my horse, could almost feel his pain, but he wouldn't let me share it. It was his alone to suffer.

I went to the Stockyards, and can't imagine I had a very good time. I can't imagine I left before last call, either.

Mister Pancakes

The grandstand at playfair. You can see the outside rail of the paddock at the very bottom of the picture. I usually watched the races from the apron just to the right of the umbrella in the lower left corner. Baldy's bench was at the end of the snake pit, about where the awning is on the building with the flat roof. I wonder who I am seeing.

This little horse was a fighter, a machine, an athlete. He cleaned up. He went right for the grain. He was still under the influence of the painkiller, and he was tired, no doubt still sore, but he was still interested, still happy to be here. At this point, everything looked fine, no outward signs of anything. Twenty four hours would tell the tale.

247

I walked him by hand a little, to the sandpit, but he wasn't up for a roll, and to the grass patch, but a bite or two was good enough. I snapped him to the hot walker while I cleaned his stall, without turning it on. He was content to stand, but his head was up, and his ears were pricked forward. I got the sense he didn't feel like he was done yet.

It was good to see, this glimmer of hope. I still didn't know enough about this game to try to look any further ahead than today, but at least I knew enough to only look that far ahead.

Marv had been through this many times before. He was proud of this little horse.

He thought they could have some fun together at the bush tracks next year, Marv always looking for a tough, honest horse to take to the bushes, the fair meets in Oregon, Washington, and Montana. Montana was always a fun trip, but I didn't know that yet. Sometimes they even took a horse or two up to Canada in the early days. Marv had talked about going back since 1972, at least.

Baldy never commented much on the bushes, but his lack of enthusiasm had more to do with his mobility than anything, is my guess. They didn't pay much in the bushes.

Twenty four critical hours passed uneventfully, and slowly and patiently, we did what we could. Officer's Citation did what he did, which was eat everything thrown his way, break his chain snaps, and make it easy to bounce out of bed quick enough to see the long shadows of the sunrise as it revealed the backstretch early in the morning.

It was a week that brought enough optimism to the stable to enter Officer's Citation in a race going a mile and seventy yards. I never figured out, and still don't know why they run at both a mile and seventy yards, and a mile and a sixteenth. The starting gate is in the same place, just to the long side of the seven-sixteenths pole on a five-furlong track. That is the black one before you get to the green three-eights pole, and as you know, it should take your horse six seconds to run from one to the other. It's amazing how much can change from one pole to the next.

We had a rider named Jerry Pruitt, who was one of the leading riders at the time. He was named on at the draw, as we had entered an open horse, no rider named. Pruitt's agent named him on the horse.

The problem is, there isn't that much to do around the barn with one horse in the stable, and if he's just walking, there is nothing to do except replace snaps on stall chains. The system was working, but we were still stress testing the snaps, and the horse wasn't winning, but the snaps were taking casualties, for sure. The guy in the tack shop was fine-tuned as far as supply and demand. A dozen brass for me, a dozen for the rest of the track. He knew how the horse felt at all times, usually showing concern if I didn't buy snaps at least once a week.

He wasn't concerned that week.

We were about half a bounce short of having our horse back. He was eating a little less, and Baldy said this was not uncommon when the season was winding down. He was feeling good.

"They'll tell you when they're ready to go home," Baldy said.

Officer's Citation wasn't ready for the pasture yet. I would take him to the grass patch every afternoon, and to the sandpit for a roll. He wasn't rolling every day, his back a little sore, no doubt. We were still keeping an eye on that knee, but for a little heat the day after a race, it seemed to be fine.

He was prescribed muscle relaxers from the vet for the back

soreness and came out of it very well going into the race.

Finally, the seventh arrived, and it was race day, Wednesday night, we were in the nightcap, and a somewhat unenthusiastic young lady at the test barn was probably going to collect some overtime pay courtesy of her favorite horse. This late in the year, all the tough horses had graduated from their condition races, so it was only going to get easier, and the Officer's Citation was coming to another peak.

I had him cleaned up when they called for the tenth that night but didn't have his bridle on yet. It prevented me from washing out. I was relaxed and very confident. He lowered his head as I slipped the bridle on, just an ordinary brown bridle, nothing flashy about it. Like an understated hood ornament on a brown sports car. Nothing fancy about either one, but classic and beautiful.

I pulled his forelock from under the forehead band.

Marv said, "Wait."

Damp spots started to form on my flanks.

"I guess nobody comin' up from the hole, Bass," Marv said. "I reckon you can take 'im up."

I took that familiar u-turn and let my horse lead us to the receiving barn. I had a fast walker tonight, taking in the sights, but not wasting any steps in getting to where we were going.

We approached the receiving barn, the last to arrive, and Marv was putting the headstall number on as we headed into the stall. Officer's Citation put his head down for Marv, and took a slow, deep breath, like a fighter before a fight. Smack the gloves together and go to battle.

"I love this little shitter," Marv said, giving him a smack on the shoulder.

He was a popular little horse.

"He ain't much," Russ Janish once said to me. And in the grand scheme of things, he wasn't. He may not have been much, but for a while he was everything to me.

He was fast enough to run with this bunch, for sure. There were a few horses in here he had beaten by a dozen lengths or more. As usual, a tough one was dropping in from somewhere higher up the ladder. It was a shame we had hooked the front runner last time because he could have done us a favor in here.

But still, if you threw out his last race, it didn't look bad. We got four to one opening line odds. The parachuter, the horse dropping in class, was the odds on favorite.

Then we were walking again, through the darkness, an occasional pool of light, yellow and muted on the way past the familiar barns, the horses in the stalls not bothering to acknowledge the cheap route horses headed to a late-season condition race. It was getting chilly, a little nip to the air. The leaves were turning, autumn was here.

We went down the six and a half furlong chute for possibly the last time this year, and by then I was a veteran in the paddock, but I still watched the man in the cowboy hat.

I looked down the stretch, past the tote board on the left, and the grandstand on the right, and could see the lights of the south hill twinkling, the radio tower lights flashing red in an up and down pattern.

A flick and a swirl of the wrist, and I'm in the saddling stall with my horse. The valet arrived with Pruitt's saddle, and a little brown Thoroughbred took a deep breath and tapped his gloves together. Officer's Citation jumped out of the stall before the riders were called, and he and I took one final circuit as instructions are misinterpreted in the paddock one more time.

Riders up! And we were headed for the track. The exchange

was smooth, and as the echo of the bugle faded, once more the white silks of the Putzier brothers adorned the rider of a good-looking Thoroughbred making his way onto the track.

I asked Baldy once why just plain white silks. The silks had black trim on the sleeves, but still, they were pretty generic even if you did get points for the understated nature.

"Easy to see," he said simply. But then he continued. "Our first year at the track, nineteen sixty, we had a good two year old named Our Buckwheat," Baldy said. "And we had white silks, but we had an M R on the back of our first set." He paused like he would, sometimes for up to ten seconds, and then continued. "Sonsabitches started calling him Mister Pancakes, and we've had plain white silks ever since."

It was always simple, but it was often multi-dimensional with the Putzier brothers.

Marv then spoke up with a commentary about the horse. "Bucky ran fifth in the futurity, beat two lengths and the rider standing up and pulling back on the reins in the win picture."

Baldy said, "He'd a got through, we win that son of a bitch easy."

I watch my cheap little horse gallop by that night in 1987 with a rider wearing plain white silks.

Whenever someone got in a little trouble in those years, Baldy was always the first to go to bat for him or any other soul on the backside who ran afoul of the rules and needed an advocate. He knew the rules better than the official issuing the sanctions, usually. For free advice on the backstretch, he was usually pretty effective in front of the stewards on judgment day.

One time that year, one of the grooms was cited for drinking alcohol and getting into a fight with someone in the parking lot across the street from the Backstretch Cafe, across Haven street. The stewards were going to suspend the groom's license, and Baldy represented him at the hearing.

He tells it, "The stewards read the charges, fighting in the barn area, and I said 'hold on. He wasn't in the barn area, or even on the property. Next charge.' Steward says to me, 'we haven't got one.' I tell the kid to take off, and the steward says to the kid, 'this is a technicality, but I'm warning you,' and I said, 'hold on. No, you aren't warning him, you are dropping the issue.' He says to me, 'you two have a nice day, Rollin.'"

The same people would chat with him every time they were in the area. It wasn't unusual for him and Jack Pring, the owner of the track, to have a long discussion on legal issues concerning the greyhound track going in across the state line, the body punch that staggered Playfair before consolidation and politics delivered the death blow.

Jack was a car salesman, and always had something pleasant to say to Baldy, who usually promptly disagreed with it.

"Isn't it a beautiful day?" Jack would say as he walked up to sell us a Toyota, or possibly just a pleasant thought.

"You see the crippled son of a bitch in front of you, Jack?" Baldy would shake his head. "I haven't had a good god damn day since 1965."

Jack would look at me and wince.

I would offer no opinions, and try unsuccessfully not to smile.

I bought a car from Jack once, a little white Toyota pick-up, extra cab, sunroof, canopy. I remember that sunroof once tumbling through space in the rearview mirror, spinning in slow motion before finally shattering on the hot pavement of US 97, the road to British Columbia, on the way to the races.

Back at Playfair, the horses were approaching the starting gate.

I could see them across the track, loading the starting gate. I watched this one with Baldy, and a cheap speed horse tried to go with the horse dropping in. The horse finished seventeen lengths behind Officer's Citation last time they faced each other, so we weren't worried about him. We hoped and wondered if he could hurt the tough horse on the front end, but he couldn't, and was done for good before they turned for home, finishing twenty-nine lengths behind the winner, the horse dropping in from the rung above. It looked like we had a chance at the quarter pole, but the other horse drew off and won by six, and we were another four lengths in front of the third-place finisher, running second for the fourth time that year.

Officer's Citation was better than the rest, but he didn't have that extra gear anymore.

We were headed back to the test barn, however, and as I picked up my horse, a familiar voice said, "Hi guys. We missed you."

He was a popular horse, my Little Provolone.

Hoofbeats

Officer's Citation had earned $2481 to this point, or an average of two hundred seventy-six dollars per start. Late in the year, earnings per start is the best, maybe the only indicator for the class of a horse. Even if they run in higher or lower classes, this is the statistic that tells the tale. For comparison's sake, Seattle Slew's average earnings per start were $71,000.

Remember dosage profiles indicating Officer's Citation could probably outrun Seattle Slew? Average earnings per start indicate how much more there is to it than the genetics. The difference is that the dosage profile is hypothetical, while earnings per start are the cold hard reality. It should be mentioned, I am not an expert on dosage profiles. I am sure there is more to it than I can explain.

And none of it matters if they back out of the feed tub, which Officer's Citation did. About half of his feed was left in the tub the morning after the race. He was sore, and it looked like we could be done for the year, which was successful, even if a little light in the win column.

It was fun, he was a fun horse, and he could set your heart on fire. But if he was hurting, there was no point in going on. The discussion was mainly where to winter, Marv's, up in Tonasket, about 200 miles away near the Canadian border, or Baldy's, about thirty miles away in Post Falls, Idaho.

Marv's was the better choice for every reason, including Baldy's physical condition. There was no hurry, however, as the meet had another two or three weeks to run, and Officer's Citation was as well off here as he was anywhere for the time being.

Another factor was that there would never be a better time to win his last condition race than right now, provided he was up for it.

After a few days, it appeared that he might be. He was back into the feed tub, most of the way, anyway. There was a race on the twenty-sixth, mile and a sixteenth, that looked like the one we could win. The muscle relaxers we would give him a day or two after the race, one time only, just to loosen the muscles a little. Once the muscles relaxed, the relaxed nature of the horse seemed to keep them that way.

The left knee was a different story. It stayed warm for a day or two, and the veterinarian was called for his opinion. His opinion was that Cortisone would be a good solution for the one remaining start. You can only go to that well so many times, and usually with diminishing results each time. I knew nothing about the process.

Baldy agreed with the assessment, and the veterinarian came over later in the morning to give Officer's Citation the Cortisone injection in his knee. I put the shank under his lip as gently as I could. We didn't want him moving with a needle in his knee joint, so we were ready with the lip chain. It was effective on Officer's Citation because he knew what it was, and he didn't want to test it.

I watched closely from the head of the horse, and Baldy watched from the stall door as the vet inserted about a two-inch long needle, maybe longer, into his left knee.

I was surprised to see blood spurt out of the needle, as though under pressure, maybe a third of a cup or so. Then the blood slowed to a small trickle, a pinkish colored liquid trickled out, and then it stopped. It seemed like a lot of blood to me, but neither Baldy nor the vet seemed concerned or surprised. The vet injected the Cortisone into the joint.

It looked like the first part of the plan was in place, and now the only question was, would it help?

The veterinarian explained to me Cortisone added elasticity and lubrication to the joint, but was temporary, and had negative consequences if overused. He gave Officer's Citation a pat on the neck as he exited the stall, and said to Baldy and me, "That should do the trick. Good luck, guys."

"We oughta be ok, Bass," Baldy said.

And, boy, were we ever. Within a day or two, I had a bully on my hands, the same one who sent chills down my spine and into my soul. He'd been hurting for a few races, and since that pain had been taken away, he looked unstoppable. Even a horse dropping in from above would run into the buzzsaw that was a healthy Officer's Citation.

Jerry Pruitt was by this time the leading rider at the meet. Jerry was a journeyman who had figured out his craft enough to be a good, steady, and consistent rider. His agent intercepted us on the way to enter, and said, "If you are going in that never won three, you're the winner, and we want the mount."

Baldy looked at me and said, "Whaddya think?"

I shrugged my shoulders, knowing it was theatrics and not a solicitation of my opinion.

"You spin me, and we will go to the stewards," Baldy said to the agent.

"We want the mount," the agent answered.

"Well, put the son of a bitch on then," Baldy said. "I'll let you handle the entry."

The agent entered the horse, and sure enough, at the draw, Pruitt was the rider.

Nothing left to do but go to the sandpit and the grass patch for four more days, and then to the track for one lap on the morning of the race.

It all went like clockwork.

We were out of shampoo, so on the morning of the race I went to the tack shop by the cafe. The owner asked as he reached for the snaps, "You want four, or a half dozen?"

"Six is the number today, chief," I said. "I need a bottle of shampoo, too."

He asked with a grin, "Are you sure?"

I didn't know what he meant. "Yeah....," I began.

He tapped his racing form, said, "I don't think you do."

Finally understanding, I laughed and said, "Maybe not, but

we can always use it at home."

I may have mentioned, at least five times previously, they shampoo the horse at the test barn when you win or run second.

He asked, "How's the horse?"

I held up the handful of snaps, looked at them and said, "Seems pretty good."

He laughed and wished me good luck. I thanked him and exited his store, feeling pretty good about life and my little horse.

It was Saturday, October 26, 1987, and it was finally getting close. We stayed away from the stall, wanting Officer's Citation to relax and stay relaxed. So far, so good.

When the eighth went to the receiving barn, and the ninth to the paddock, I got the hoof pick, Hooflex and mane card, touched up the hooves and brushed his mane and tail. He was looking and feeling good and I was alert for one of his sudden leaps, but he stayed relatively cool. I gave him a quick wipe down with the rag and was putting his bridle on when they made the call.

"Attention horsemen, bring your horses to the receiving barn for the tenth race. Horses to the receiving barn for the tenth."

Marv looked at me, and I said, "Wait." He gave me a nod and a wink.

I could smell the straw, a little bit musty, a little bit dusty in the chilly October air. I led Officer's Citation out of the stall, very alert, ready for him. He took a breath, puffed up his chest a little, and strolled out of the stall. I gave him a pat on the neck as we turned toward the paved pathway.

When Officer's Citation hit the pathway, he shifted gears and I had a faster walker than I had led over in a couple of months. We were picked to win by every handicapper in the form, and the program. On paper, it was his easiest race, at his best distance. It was a good one to finish on.

I took it all in going to the receiving barn, and even the neighbor who never looked all that happy, said, "Good luck, kid." It may have been the most we said to each other to that point since she found me stretched out on the straw bale several weeks ago.

I can hear the sounds, even, as I look back. The trees were losing leaves, and some of the stalls were empty, the meet winding down. We went to the receiving barn and straight to the stall, where Marv put the headstall number on and Officer's Citation surveyed his competition.

I didn't point any competitors out to him, and he didn't look like he was sweating any of them.

We heard a distant cheer from the grandstand, and the PA crackled to life; " Attention, horsemen, bring your horses to the paddock for the tenth race. Horses to the paddock for the tenth."

We began the walk over. It was the part I always enjoyed most, going through the quiet part of the barn area around the north end. It was like the calm before the storm as we walked through the shadows and isolated pools of low-level light. You could smell a little wood smoke in the air, a smell that reminded me of autumn in the Palouse, bonfires and Friday night football. We were the number one horse, so we led the way down the chute and into the paddock.

Officer's Citation and I both had a bounce to our step, almost a strut, as we made our way down the six and a half furlong chute to the gap at the paddock. I watched the hand do its circle, Marv directing the show as usual. I headed Officer's Citation out, and he was saddled, no problems, and I went for another circuit or two, taking the widest possible route. The other horses already looked beaten if you noticed their body language.

Finally, the riders were out, the riders were up, and we led them to the ponies as the bugle sounded the call to post. They paraded past the grandstand, made the turn, galloped slowly to the backstretch, and then began to enter the starting gate.

The odds on Officer's Citation were seven to two, making him the slight favorite. He looked the part. I bet twenty dollars to win only, It was all I had with me. I went out to watch the race beside Baldy, who was standing at the rail by the eighth pole, my lucky spot. I didn't know where Marv and Carol were, and I don't remember seeing Deke at all that night, but he must have been there.

The horses were loaded into the starting gate quickly and the PA boomed, "Flag is up, they're all in line."

"There they go!"

It was a good start, and as they went into the far turn the first time, the cheap speed horse from our last race went to the front. We had beaten him by a combined total of forty lengths in the two races we ran against him. He was setting slow fractions, but he was running all out. I was certain he would collapse when the running started for real at the quarter pole.

They stayed strung out past the grandstand the first time, and nothing looked like they were under a hold. Just like this, and we were golden. They stayed in line through the backstretch. A few of the closers trying to wind up, but the pace was too slow. They weren't moving forward quickly enough to be a threat to Officer's Citation, who was under a stranglehold, running second as they passed the three-eighths pole.

We were going to win this one for fun, and we were a quarter mile from home in our last race of the year. The horse on the front end was beginning to falter, and as Officer's Citation galloped into the turn he was two lengths behind and taking dead aim at the leader.

And in one hammer of a hoofbeat, my world came to an end.

The end of the world brings forth visions of thunder, lightning, and hurricanes—visions of the earth erupting and the heavens falling. Within these visions, I can see the silhouette of a little brown Thoroughbred. But it is a clear and crisp night in late October and the storm is imagined; only the silhouette is real.

The end began with weakness in a bone that corresponds roughly to the human wrist. It all started with a bone chip, A tiny micro-fracture. A nine-hundred-pound athlete running nearly forty miles an hour changes leads, and the algebra of weight and velocity conspire. It is more than the knee can take this time, and it is the end of my little brown Thoroughbred.

A snap, a gasp, and a grunt, it all happens so fast. No one hears a whinny or a scream. The rider stands up in the irons and hauls back on the reins, dangerously close to catastrophe himself. Three hops and a sudden stop later, we've gone from two back and dead aim, to dead horse and too bad for him.

In the end, I am left with echoes of an agonized and haunting groan, a bewildered animal suffering his pain with quiet and humble dignity.

We tell ourselves they love to run, and we know it to be true. It's a thin line, like a tiny stress fracture. A tiny margin, like a wafer-thin bone chip. The little things turn out to be the big things. They love to run, and it can break them. When they break, it will kill them. If you aren't careful, they can hurt you. If they love you, it can kill you just as dead.

Baldy's voice drifts through the fog, "You better get over there…"

I don't ever want to get there, but I run as fast as I can. The horses are strung out on the track from avoiding Officer's Citation. As I run across the infield toward the quarter pole, I can see him leaning against the outrider's horse. Nothing about the picture looks right.

No one will look me in the eye, except for him. I have no choice but to meet his bewildered gaze. I owe him so much more than that. It surprises me, but I can see the fire still burns deep within. He still believes he will live to see tomorrow.

All these years later, I still don't know what to say. Thousands of words I write, and all I can think, all I can feel, is, I'm sorry. I am so very sorry, my Little Provolone, for what has become of you.

What have I done to you?

I lean against that powerful chest of his, trying to make that leg straighten, but I can't. It's bending the wrong way; I can't make it stop bending the wrong way. His ears are pricked forward the way they always are. He's a kind little horse, he's never hurt a soul, and he looks across the neck of the outrider's horse as the tractor pulls up, dragging a box on wheels that says horse ambulance.

I used to call it the meat wagon.

Marv has his hand on my shoulder. He applies a little pressure and eases me out of the way.

Officer's Citation passes the quarter pole one last time, his nose nearly touching the ground as he struggles into the ambulance, all of us trying to help. His ears are still pricked forward, twitching back and forth; he is in pain but curious, wondering what happens next. I don't have the heart to tell him what is to be his tragic fate. I want to trade places with him, but It doesn't work that way.

There is nothing left to do but pick up his bridle tomorrow morning at the test barn. He's the one who schools me to the test barn, shows me how it works, how peaceful it is late at night when all the other racehorses are back in the barn. Those times when just the three of us, Officer's Citation and I, and a reluctant young woman anxiously wait for the best moments of my life to gallop on by.

I place my hand upon his back and trace my fingertips over his body for the last time.

I wish he'd have kicked me.

Marv leans back against the rail and studies his youngest son, the one who never cared much for horses.

"Colin," he says.

It must be serious, calling me Colin.

"Baldy's waiting up't the cafe."

****

Sometimes I find myself next to the rail on the backstretch in the still air of an early spring morning, and I hear those muted hoofbeats. I swear I can see a little brown Thoroughbred, his head bowed, his coat slick and shining, slow galloping toward me from somewhere out there in the mist. I'm sure I'll be able to see him clearly, any second now...

The End

Epilogue

Marv and Carol for many years could be found having some fun at one bush track or another, from British Columbia to Montana, Oregon, and Washington. Marv passed away after having surgery for a heart valve replacement in 2004.

Carol's health deteriorated from that day forward, and she passed away a few years later in 2010 from diabetes complications.

Baldy stayed active in local politics and remained a champion and advocate for the underdog until he passed away in 1997, approximately 40 years after he was told he had about a year to live.

Guy played five years in the NFL, and passed away in April of 2018, from health problems associated with life in the National Football League.

Deke went to the track for a few years. He saddled some winners at Emerald Downs, Exhibition Park, and a few bush tracks in Montana. He is a general contractor in the Seattle area.

Judy is living near her daughter Mary in Huntsville, Alabama.

Leonard is in Montana.

About the Author

Colin Putzier is a fan of horseracing, and a freelance photographer. He was the track photographer at Sundowns Race Track in Kennewick in 2017 and 2018. He has also worked as a video camera operator at various small tracks in the northwest, and was fortunate enough to be the track photographer at Bluegrass Downs in Paducah, Kentucky, from 2014-15. If you didn't find him shooting video or taking pictures at a racetrack during those years, he was either screwing up your retail experience, or painting your neighbor's house. Like any other house painter, he still dreams of winning the Belmont Stakes.

You can connect with me on:

 https://www.facebook.com/cole.putzier

Made in the USA
Coppell, TX
02 May 2020

23916273R00162